The Nexus™ Framework for Scaling Scrum

The Nexus™ Framework for Scaling Scrum

CONTINUOUSLY DELIVERING AN INTEGRATED PRODUCT WITH MULTIPLE SCRUM TEAMS

Kurt Bittner

Patricia Kong

Dave West

PRENTICE
HALL

Boston • Columbus • Indianapolis • New York • San Francisco • Amsterdam • Cape Town
Dubai • London • Madrid • Milan • Munich • Paris • Montreal • Toronto • Delhi • Mexico City
São Paulo • Sydney • Hong Kong • Seoul • Singapore • Taipei • Tokyo

For information about buying this title in bulk quantities, or for special sales opportunities (which may include electronic versions; custom cover designs; and content particular to your business, training goals, marketing focus, or branding interests), please contact our corporate sales department at corpsales@pearsoned.com or (800) 382-3419.

For government sales inquiries, please contact governmentsales@pearsoned.com.

For questions about sales outside the U.S., please contact intlcs@pearson.com.

Visit us on the Web: informit.com/aw

Library of Congress Control Number: 2017956213

ISBN-13: 978-0-13-468266-2
ISBN-10: 0-13-468266-1

1 17

To the members of the community of Professional Scrum Trainers, from whom we learn every day.

CONTENTS

FOREWORD

This book is excellent. It begins with a simple application of Nexus. It then describes its application in increasingly complex situations. The authors lay out the complexities, the problems they cause, and how one can apply Nexus to address them. They thread the ideas together with a case study. This is backed up by The Nexus Guide, the definitive body of knowledge.

But, why does Nexus even exist?

Scrum is a framework within which a team of people can address a complex problem to create an increment of value within a short period of time. Over 27 years, Scrum has proven its value in many applications.

However, Scrum is only designed for a single team. Situations often call for multiple teams with different capabilities to work together to create value. Organizations naturally want to build on the initial Scrum framework.

Over the years, I have worked with hundreds of organizations, adhering to the framework and values of Scrum while scaling its use to tens, hundreds, and even thousands of people working together to create a single outcome.

Many other Scrum practitioners have also done so. To the degree that we applied our prior knowledge, much of the productivity and value of Scrum was retained.

Based on my experiences and those of others that I work with in Scrum.org, I designed a defined framework for using many Scrum teams on a single product or problem. The result is Nexus, an exoskeleton that rests on top of many Scrum teams. Nexus provides information and management information for guiding their working together. As much productivity as possible is retained, methods of increasing productivity are described, and remediation techniques for resolving failures are included.

Read and learn more. Scrum on.

—Ken Schwaber

PREFACE

Our goal in writing this book was simple: to expose people already familiar with Scrum to a simple yet powerful way to apply the same Scrum concepts with which they are familiar to Products that demand the efforts of more than one team. More than 12 million people use Scrum every day, and many of those people work on large multi-team efforts. Nexus evolved to meet the needs of these people, and although it is being used by many organizations, no book describing it yet existed. We hope that the readers of this book will be able to apply use Nexus to scale, and perhaps even improve, their Scrum practices. As we like to say, "Scaled Scrum is still Scrum."

WHO SHOULD READ THIS BOOK

Anyone who uses Scrum will benefit from reading this book, because at some point you will find that a single Scrum Team is no longer sufficient to deliver your Product. Adding teams sounds easy, but unmanaged inter-team dependencies quickly overwhelm a merely intuitive approach. This book will help every team member understand Nexus better. Beyond the Scrum Teams, stakeholders for Scrum Teams will find this book helpful in understanding the challenges that multi-team efforts face, and it will help them to better support the teams with whom they work.

HOW THIS BOOK IS ORGANIZED

This book assumes that you are already familiar with the Scrum Framework and builds on that knowledge by explaining how to scale Scrum to develop a large product using Nexus.

Chapter 1, "Introduction to Scaling Agile," does just that. It introduces you to the use of Agile in contexts that require more than one Scrum team working on a project.

Chapter 2, "Introducing Nexus," focuses on the basic principles and concepts behind Nexus, including when you need a Nexus and what you need to get started.

Chapter 3, "Forming a Nexus," focuses on how to form a Nexus around a product, even if that product is still only an idea without a team. For existing products and teams, we describe how to add teams while creating a Nexus. We also describe how you can organize the Scrum Teams in the Nexus and how to identify (and minimize) Product Backlog dependencies.

Chapter 4, "Planning in Nexus," focuses on organizing the work of the Nexus: soliciting, refining, and validating a large backlog against business objectives; setting goals; and planning the Sprint.

Chapter 5, "Running a Sprint in Nexus," focuses on the work of the Nexus during the Sprint: working with the Nexus Sprint Backlog, running the Nexus Daily Scrum, conducting Nexus Sprint Reviews, and conducting the Nexus Sprint Retrospective.

Chapter 6, "Evolving the Nexus," focuses on managing the Nexus, including reporting progress, improving performance and throughput, and removing bottlenecks.

Chapter 7, "The Nexus in Emergency Mode," focuses on how Nexus helps organizations overcome typical scaling challenges, including helping distributed teams work better together and responding to challenges that keep teams from working together effectively.

Chapter 8, "Retrospective on the Nexus Journey," reflects on the typical journey that teams and organizations take when they scale Scrum. It looks at how the elements of Nexus help them on that journey, the typical challenges they face, and how they can overcome those challenges. It also looks ahead at things they can do to continue their journey of improving their ability to deliver complex applications.

Register your copy of *The Nexus™ Framework for Scaling Scrum* on the InformIT site for convenient access to updates and/or corrections as they become available. To start the registration process, go to informit.com/register and log in or create an account. Enter the product ISBN (9780134682662) and click Submit. Look on the Registered Products tab for an Access Bonus Content link next to this product, and follow that link to access any available bonus materials. If you would like to be notified of exclusive offers on new editions and updates, please check the box to receive email from us.

ACKNOWLEDGMENTS

We had a lot of help and support in writing this book. First, we have to thank Ken and Christina Schwaber for their support, encouragement, and perspective on how Nexus evolved from Scrum, and to thank Ken Schwaber and Jeff Sutherland for creating Scrum itself, upon which Nexus is based. The Nexus Framework exists because a collaborative team of people came together to translate their experiences into something that could be shared with everyone in the form of The Nexus Guide.

We are also indebted to the Professional Scrum Trainer community, whose members shared their valuable time helping to improve the book through their thoughtful suggestions and painstaking reviews. For their extensive contributions, our deepest gratitude goes to Peter Götz, Jesse Houwing, Richard Hundhausen, Ralph Jocham, Mikkel Toudal Kristiansen, Rob Maher, Jeronimo Palacios, and Steve Porter. Our thanks also extend to Eric Naiburg, whose careful writer's eye helped us to express ideas more simply and effectively, and to Sabrina Love, who designed our cover.

Finally, this book would not be possible without the support we received from the team at Pearson/Addison-Wesley, notably our editor, Chris Guzikowski;

our development editor, Chris Zahn; our production editor, Julie Nahil; and our copy editor, Stephanie Geels, all of whom helped us to refine and publish the work you are reading.

—Kurt, Patricia, and Dave

ABOUT THE AUTHORS

Kurt Bittner has more than 35 years of experience helping teams to deliver software in short feedback-driven cycles, as a developer, as a product manager and product owner, as an industry analyst, and as an organizational change agent. He is the author of three other books on software engineering and many blogs and articles, and he is a frequent speaker at conferences.

Patricia Kong is a key contributor to the Nexus Framework and the Evidence-Based Management framework. She led product development, product management, and marketing for several early-stage companies in the U.S. and Europe, and she worked in business development and engagement management for Forrester Research. She is fluent in four languages.

Dave West is the CEO and Product Owner at Scrum.org. He is a frequent keynote speaker at major industry conferences and is a widely read author of books, blogs, articles, and research reports. He has led both product development and consulting organizations for multinational organizations.

INTRODUCTION TO SCALING AGILE

Agile software development has, to use the term popularized by Geoffrey Moore, *crossed the chasm*.[1] No one today has a serious conversation about whether Agile software development is relevant; today's conversations are focused on when and where to use it. At large organizations, those conversations often turn to questions of scale: No one questions whether agile approaches work well for a single small, co-located team, but they do question whether the approach can be used to develop and deliver large products built by many teams.

This book is about scaling Scrum using an approach called Nexus, developed by one of the co-creators of Scrum. In the course of the book, we will discuss why scaling is hard and how to overcome its challenges. This brief chapter sets the scene, explaining why Agile is important, why Scrum is important, and why Nexus is the simplest and, we think, the best way to scale Scrum.

---

1. https://www.forbes.com/sites/danschawbel/2013/12/17/geoffrey-moore-why-crossing-the-chasm-is-still-relevant/#123c4f95782d

WHY AGILE?

Agile software delivery practices are hardly new. Scrum is now more than 20 years old,[2] and the Agile Manifesto was signed more than 15 years ago.[3] What is new is that software has become a disruptive force in every industry, and organizations have turned to agile approaches to enable them to deliver innovative software-based solutions.[4]

Agile software delivery practices enable teams to deliver more business value more quickly by improving collaboration and using an empirical process to inspect, adapt, and improve business results. In today's competitive business environment, long-term planning and multiyear projects have given way to frequent releases. Agile's inspect-and-adapt approach fits the bill.

WHY SCRUM?

According to Forrester Research, 90% of Agile teams use Scrum.[5] Key to this popularity is the fact that Scrum is not prescriptive but is a framework based on a set of principles and values, consisting of three roles (Product Owner, Scrum Master, and Development Team), five events (the Sprint, Sprint Planning, the Daily Scrum, the Sprint Review, and the Sprint Retrospective), and three artifacts (the Product Backlog, the Sprint Backlog, and the Product Increment), making it highly adaptable to different situations.[6]

Scrum's strength is that it is simple. It focuses on a single team producing a single product. It has only three roles: a Product Owner, focused on business goals; a Development Team, who develops the product; and a Scrum Master who helps the Product Owner and the Development Team achieve those

---

2. https://kenschwaber.wordpress.com/2015/11/22/scrum-development-kit/

3. http://agilemanifesto.org

4. Venture capitalist Marc Andreessen famously opined that "software is eating the world," a reference to the accelerating trend of small software-based startups taking down their much larger, more established, better financed, entrenched competitors. See http://www.wsj.com/articles/SB10001424053111903480904576512250915629460 for the full article.

5. https://www.forrester.com/How+Can+You+Scale+Your+Agile+Adoption/fulltext/-/E-res110444#AST962998 2013

6. To read more about Scrum, see http://www.scrumguides.org/scrum-guide.html.

objectives by teaching, coaching, and facilitating, among other things. Although Scrum is easy to understand, mastery still requires commitment and dedication to break old habits and establish new ones.

WHAT IS A PRODUCT?

Many organizations are still accustomed to thinking in terms of *projects*. A project is an initiative with a finite length, a well-defined beginning, a specific scope to deliver, and usually a defined end date.

In contrast, a *product* is long-lived, often with no defined end. Using projects to deliver and support products results in many problems, not the least of which is a tendency for stakeholders to pile on requirements due to uncertainty about whether there will ever be a "next" release. In most organizations, projects are seen as sources of cost, whereas products are seen as sources of business value. Transitioning from project development to product development will often change the perception of what development teams do from merely supporting the business to being an active driver of the business.

If the product is worth developing, it needs to be funded and managed differently. Products require regular releases to meeting the ever-changing needs of product users. Products require a dedicated team to build and support the product across a series of releases, and they require that there is no difference between maintenance, new development, and enhancements from a product team perspective.

WHAT IS SCRUM?

Scrum is a framework that helps teams overcome complex adaptive problems to deliver a product with the highest possible value. Many organizations have successfully used Scrum, starting in the early 1990s.

Scrum is founded on empirical process control theory, or empiricism. Empiricism asserts that knowledge comes from experience and from making decisions based on what is known. Scrum employs an iterative, incremental approach to optimize predictability and control risk through continuous learning. Three pillars uphold every implementation of empirical process control: *transparency*, *inspection*, and *adaptation*. There are more than 12 million Scrum practitioners, and the numbers grow daily.[7]

Although it is possible to use some Scrum techniques for projects, Scrum is fundamentally focused on *product* development.

The basic elements of the Scrum Framework are depicted in Figure 1-1.[8]

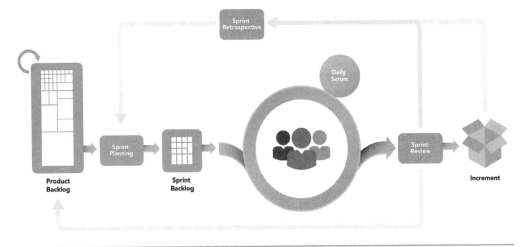

Figure 1-1 The Scrum Framework

There are realistic limits to what a single Scrum Team can achieve, however. Organizations may be tempted to simply add more people to the team or more teams to the product to achieve higher velocity, but decades of practical experience have shown this to be counterproductive.[9]

---

7. Scrum.org.

8. The Scrum framework is documented in the Scrum Guide, which is available, free of charge, at http://www.scrumguides.org/.

9. This was described in Fred Brooks' classic work, *The Mythical Man-Month: Essays on Software Engineering*, in the context of traditional software projects. Agile approaches don't change the basic problem: increasing team size causes an exponential increase in communication complexity that defeats any productivity gains beyond a practical maximum of 7±2 team members. The FBI Sentinel case study is also instructive: http://www.scrumcasestudies.com/fbi/.

WHY NEXUS?

Some products—and some would argue, most products—are too complex to be delivered by a single Scrum Team. Examples of these include automobiles or other physical products with combinations of hardware and software, or very complex software products that require the coordinated efforts of many Scrums Teams to deliver. Other products have time-to-market pressures that require more capabilities to be delivered in a short period of time than one team can deliver.

Faced with these challenges, organizations need more than one Scrum Team to work on a single product. Multiple Scrum Teams working together to build a single product often struggle to create "done" integrated work every Sprint because of the added complexity of dependencies at scale. Signs that complexity is overwhelming effective product delivery include individual teams presenting their individual increments instead of an integrated product at the Sprint Review, or when they require a series of "hardening" Sprints to deal with accumulated technical debt, or when an integration team is required to bring together the work of other teams.

The Nexus Framework helps to solve this by enabling organizations to plan, launch, scale, and manage larger product development initiatives (especially those that involve substantial software development) using Scrum. Nexus enables multiple Scrum Teams working on a single product to come together as a single larger unit, called a Nexus.

A Nexus can be thought of as a kind of "exoskeleton" that protects and strengthens Scrum Teams by simplifying and managing the connections and dependencies between them, and by providing transparent bottom-up insight into how the teams are working together. The foundation of a Nexus is to encourage transparency and communication to keep scaling as uniform as possible. With Nexus, scaling Scrum to larger, more complex products is still Scrum.

SIMPLICITY IS THE KEY TO SCALING

The key to scaling agile to work across many teams is reduce or eliminate dependencies between those teams. Nexus provides a simple set of extensions to Scrum to help teams do just that. In the coming chapters, we'll describe those extensions, as well as complementary practices, that help organizations deliver better products, more effectively. After a brief description of Nexus in the next chapter, the remainder of the book will focus on exploring different aspects of Nexus through a case study. And without further introduction, let's jump into Nexus.

INTRODUCING 2 NEXUS

In this chapter, we describe the Nexus Framework in its entirety. As you will see, Nexus is a relatively small and simple extension of Scrum. As we like to say, "Scaled Scrum is still Scrum." Scrum itself is quite simple, at least to understand. When scaling, this simplicity is a big advantage because complexity is the enemy of scaling. Nexus' simplicity also makes it highly adaptable, as we will see in subsequent chapters.

What Is Nexus?

Nexus is a framework that enables multiple Scrum Teams to collaboratively work from a single Product Backlog to deliver at least one "Done" Integrated Increment every Sprint. "Multiple" means, typically, three to nine Scrum teams. Why not two? Because two teams can generally coordinate between one another without additional structure. Why nine? Just as Scrum recommends limiting teams to no more than nine members to improve cohesion and reduce complexity, Nexus recommends the same for the number of teams. Just as in Scrum, however, this upper limit is not absolute and slightly larger numbers may still work, depending on the circumstances. With Nexus we have discovered that collaboration complexity and coordination between teams increases significantly beyond nine teams, and for those cases some different techniques apply.[1]

Since Nexus builds on Scrum, its parts will be familiar to those who have used Scrum. The difference is that more attention is paid to dependencies and communication between Scrum Teams (see Figure 2-1).

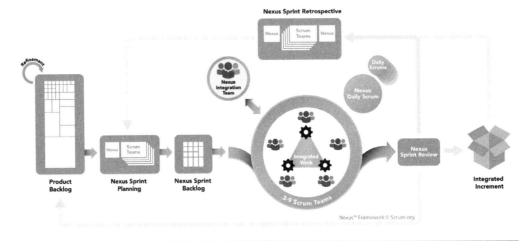

Figure 2-1 The Nexus Framework for scaling Scrum

NEXUS EXTENDS SCRUM

Nexus is Scrum, with some small additions (see Table 2-1).

- **It adds one additional Artifact: the Nexus Sprint Backlog.** Nexus Sprint Backlog is the Nexus' plan for the Sprint; it helps the Nexus understand what Scrum Teams are working on and makes any dependencies transparent that may exist between the teams during the Sprint.

---

1. George Miller's oft-cited paper, "The Magical Number Seven, Plus or Minus Two: Some Limits on Our Capacity for Processing Information," describes limitations in the way that we process information and form memories that reinforces ad hoc experience in organizing teams: when teams grow beyond about nine people they begin to lose cohesion and their work becomes harder to manage. For more information on Miller's article, see https://en.wikipedia.org/wiki/The_Magical_Number_Seven,_Plus_or_Minus_Two.

- **It adds five additional Events: Refinement, Nexus Sprint Planning, the Nexus Daily Scrum, the Nexus Sprint Review, and the Nexus Sprint Retrospective.** These additional events extend Scrum to ensure that work is divided and coordinated across Scrum Teams in the most effective manner possible, and to share experiences across teams in the Nexus.

- **It removes the individual Scrum Team Sprint Review, in favor of the Nexus Sprint Review.** Since Scrum Teams in a Nexus work together to produce a single Integrated Increment, that Integrated Increment should be reviewed as a whole.

- **It adds a new Role: the Nexus Integration Team.** The Nexus Integration Team (NIT) exists to promote and provide transparent accountability for integration in a Nexus. It coaches and guides the application of Nexus with the Scrum Teams as well as within the organization. The NIT consists of the Product Owner of the product, a Scrum Master, and NIT members who are usually members of the Scrum Teams in the Nexus, but may come from other functional areas in the organization such as Operations, Security, Architecture, or other specialist areas that may help the Nexus deliver an Integrated Increment. These "outside" members may be temporary members who join the NIT for as long as is necessary.

Table 2-1 Nexus Roles, Events, and Artifacts

Roles	Events	Artifacts
Development Teams	The Sprint	Product Backlog
Product Owner	*Nexus Sprint Planning* *	*Nexus Sprint Backlog* *
Scrum Master	Sprint Planning	Sprint Backlog
Nexus Integration Team *	*Nexus Daily Scrum* *	Integrated Increment
	Daily Scrum	
	Nexus Sprint Review *	
	Nexus Sprint Retrospective *	
	Sprint Retrospective	
	Refinement *	

* Nexus specific

THE NEXUS INTEGRATION TEAM

The NIT ensures that an Integrated Increment is produced at least every Sprint for the Nexus. The Scrum Teams do the work. Ultimately, the NIT is accountable for maximizing the value of the integrated Product (see Figure 2-2). Their activities may include developing tools and practices that will help with integration or serving as coaches and consultants to help with coordination.

NIT members need to have a teaching mind-set to help Scrum Teams resolve their issues whenever possible. Their role is to help to highlight issues that need to be solved and to help the Scrum Teams solve the issues. Only in emergencies does the NIT jump in and solve problems directly.

The NIT consists of:

- **The Product Owner,** *the* owner of the Product, and ultimately accountable for its success. In the context of the NIT, the Product Owner is accountable for ensuring that maximum value is delivered by the Nexus during each Sprint. The Product Owner's role does not change from Scrum; the scope of the work is simply more complex.
- **A Scrum Master,** who has overall responsibility for ensuring the Nexus framework is enacted and understood. This Scrum Master is often a Scrum Master in one or more of the other Scrum Teams in the Nexus.
- **A Development Team,** whose members are usually members of Scrum Teams in the Nexus.

Contrary to what its name may suggest, the NIT doesn't integrate the work of all Scrum Teams as it is delivered. Instead, it is accountable for ensuring that the teams are able to achieve integration themselves.

Members coach Scrum Teams and help remove dependencies. If something is preventing the Scrum Teams in the Nexus from producing an integrated Product, the NIT is accountable for making sure that those issues get resolved.

Product Owner
Accountable for maximizing the value of the Product

Development Team
Accountable for creating Integrated Increments that are "Done"

Scrum Master
Accountable for the Scrum Teams doing Scrum and
Nexus correctly and maximizing the value delivered by
the Development Team

Figure 2-2 The NIT is accountable for maximizing the value of the integrated Product

Members of the NIT may also work on Scrum Teams in the Nexus, but when
they do they must put their work on the NIT first for the greater benefit the
whole Nexus (see Figure 2-3).

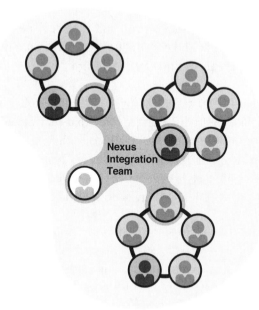

Figure 2-3 Members of the NIT are usually drawn from Scrum Teams

NIT members may come from outside the Scrum Teams; that is, from other parts of the organization. When they do, it is to provide unique expertise that the Scrum Teams lack, in areas such as Enterprise Architecture or Continuous Delivery, or in some area of specialized domain knowledge. NIT members may simply obtain their help without them actually becoming full-fledged members of the Nexus, but in some cases, when extensive support is needed, it may make sense for them to actually join the Nexus. When they do, they become accountable for Product delivery, just as are other members of the NIT.

The membership of the NIT can change over time as its needs evolve. Early in the life cycle of a Nexus, it may focus on coaching the Scrum Teams in the Nexus on scaling practices, or it may be more involved in stabilizing the shared build and test automation framework. Later in the life cycle, when the Nexus is running smoothly, the NIT may shift to raising awareness of issues from cross-team dependencies. Chapter 3, "Forming a Nexus," describes the formation, composition, and evolution of the NIT in more detail.

NEXUS EVENTS

Nexus adds four events to Scrum, and replaces one Scrum event, to help Scrum Teams divide and coordinate work across teams in the most effective manner.[2] The events defined by Nexus are

- **Refinement** is a formal event for the Nexus to collaborate on the details of the Product Backlog Items (PBIs) and see that they are adequately independent, so that the teams can select and work on without excessive conflict. In the process of working out the dependencies, teams also work out which backlog items they will likely work on. The Nexus continually refines the Product Backlog, as needed, and there is no specific time box for refinement.

---

2. Nexus events are guided by the time boxes for their related Scrum events, meaning that they generally take a similar amount of time. As a practical matter, a Nexus event takes as much time as the Nexus needs and is over when it's over. If, after that, the Nexus thinks that it took too long, there is a good opportunity for inspection and adaptation to improve for the next time.

- **Nexus Sprint Planning** helps the teams in the Nexus to collectively agree on the Nexus Goal and how each team will contribute to it.
- **The Nexus Daily Scrum** helps the Nexus to make integration issues transparent so that the Scrum Teams can know who is responsible for fixing them. It is a daily opportunity for the teams in the Nexus to sync with one another.
- **The Nexus Sprint Review** enables the Nexus to gather feedback on the Integrated Increment. It replaces individual Scrum Team Sprint Reviews.
- **The Nexus Sprint Retrospective** helps the teams share experiences and coordinate their resolution of shared challenges.

REFINEMENT

In Scrum, Product Backlog refinement is not a mandatory event, but it is a strongly recommended practice. In Nexus, refinement is essential; it helps Scrum Teams work together to determine which team will deliver specific PBIs and to identify cross-dependencies across teams. Refinement is a cross-team event, with as many Scrum Team members present as is necessary to understand and decompose the PBIs.

Refinement results in a Product Backlog that is granular enough for Scrum Teams to pull work without creating unmanageable dependencies. During Refinement, the Scrum Teams should focus on these questions.

- What work will each team pull?
- In what order does that work need to be done to deliver the greatest business value earliest, while minimizing risk and complexity?

NEXUS SPRINT PLANNING

The Nexus takes the refined Product Backlog as input for the Nexus Sprint Planning event (see Figure 2-4). Nexus Sprint Planning helps to synchronize the activities of the Scrum Teams in a Nexus for a single Sprint.

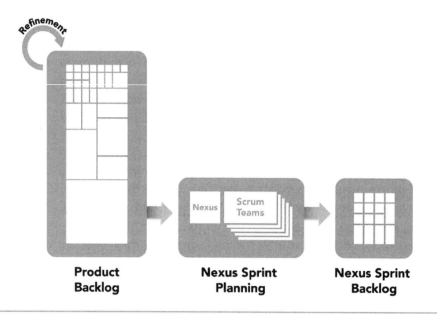

Figure 2-4 Nexus Sprint Planning

Nexus Sprint Planning consists of:

- **Validating the Product Backlog.** The Scrum Teams review the PBIs and make any necessary adjustments needed to the work from the Refinement event. All of the Scrum Teams should participate and contribute to minimize communication issues; however, only the appropriate representatives (those who feel that they can make a contribution to refining the PBIs) from each of the Scrum Teams need to attend.

- **Formulating the Nexus Goal.** The Nexus Goal is a Sprint objective that is met through the implementation of PBIs by multiple teams.

- **Scrum Team Sprint Planning.** Once the Nexus Goal for the Sprint is understood, each Scrum Team will conduct its individual Sprint Planning events in which the members create their own Sprint Backlogs. As they identify dependencies with other teams, they work with those teams to minimize or eliminate the dependencies.

  In some cases, this will mean that the sequence of work across teams may have to be adjusted to let one team finish its work before another starts.

This could be accomplished by breaking apart dependent work so that some parts can be worked independently, or by one team choosing non-dependent PBIs to work on, to avoid waste resulting from unresolved cross-team dependencies. Teams may also work together to shift work from one team to another to better balance the work. The NIT will help to make sure that dependencies are communicated and visualized on the Nexus Sprint Backlog.

Nexus Sprint Planning is complete when each Scrum Team in the Nexus has finished its individual Sprint Planning events.

THE NEXUS DAILY SCRUM

The Nexus Daily Scrum brings together the appropriate representatives from individual Scrum Teams to inspect the current state of the Integrated Increment and to identify integration issues or newly discovered cross-team dependencies. Topics typically discussed include the following.

- Was the previous day's work successfully integrated, and if not, why?
- Have any new dependencies been identified?
- What information needs to be shared across teams in the Nexus?

During the Nexus Daily Scrum and throughout the day, the Nexus Sprint Backlog may be updated by the Scrum Teams to visualize and manage current inter-team dependencies. It is not simply an aggregation of the individual teams' Sprint Backlogs, since each team will have work for itself as well as the Product Backlog work that it needs to do. Work that is identified during the Nexus Daily Scrum is then taken back to individual Scrum Teams for planning inside their Daily Scrum events.

THE NEXUS SPRINT REVIEW

The Nexus Sprint Review replaces individual Scrum Team Sprint Reviews and is held at the end of the Sprint. Its purpose is to capture feedback from stakeholders on the entire Integrated Increment of the Nexus. The Nexus Sprint Review replaces the individual Scrum Team Sprint Reviews because individual Scrum Teams might not produce a meaningful Integrated Increment on their own when Nexus is used.

There are several benefits to having a single Sprint Review for the Nexus, including the following.

- Teams are logically each other's stakeholders, so they can provide one another with feedback that helps the Nexus improve.
- If individual Scrum Team Sprint Reviews were held, stakeholders may not be able to attend all of them, and even if they did they would not see the integrated Product.
- Some issues only become evident when the integrated Product is reviewed as a whole, especially when each team is developing one or more components. Each component may work in isolation, but they may not work together to produce an integrated Product.
- Reviewing the Integrated Increment as a whole brings all the teams in the Nexus together and reminds them that their goal is a single integrated solution.

Even when some teams may actually deliver logically separated subproducts that may be independently reviewed, shipped, and used, there is value in reviewing them in the context of the Nexus' integrated Product Increment.

All members of the Nexus participate in the Nexus Sprint Review.

THE NEXUS SPRINT RETROSPECTIVE

The Nexus Sprint Retrospective provides the means by which the Nexus enables inspection and adaptation. To conduct the Nexus Retrospective:

1. Representatives from across the Nexus meet and identify issues that have impeded more than a single team to make shared issues transparent to all Scrum Teams. The representatives consist of the NIT members, as well as anyone with an interest in sharing their perspectives on inter-team issues.

2. Each Scrum Team holds its own Sprint Retrospective, just as they would do in Scrum, but the team also considers issues raised from the first part of the Nexus Retrospective as input to its team discussions while the members determine actions to address these issues.

3. Representatives from the Scrum Teams meet once again to discuss common issues identified in the Scrum Team Retrospectives. They agree on how to visualize and track the identified actions that will enable the Nexus to learn and adapt as a whole.

QUESTIONS TO ASK IN EVERY NEXUS SPRINT RETROSPECTIVE

Nearly every Nexus encounters common scaling challenges. Questions that help teams to identify challenges include the following.

- Was any work left undone?
- Did the Nexus generate technical debt?
- Were all artifacts, particularly code, frequently (as often as every day) successfully integrated?
- Was the software successfully built, tested, and deployed often enough to prevent the overwhelming accumulation of unresolved dependencies?

When challenges are identified, ask the following:

- Why did this happen?
- How can technical debt be undone?
- How can the recurrence be prevented?

Nexus Events are described in more detail in Chapter 5, "Nexus in Action."

NEXUS ARTIFACTS

Artifacts capture the results of work performed. They also provide transparency and opportunities for inspection and adaptation.

PRODUCT BACKLOG

There is a single Product Backlog for the entire Nexus and all of its Scrum Teams. Since a Nexus is organized a single product, it only has a single Product Owner, and that single Product Owner maintains a single Product Backlog. All teams pull work from this single artifact.

Nexus Goal

During the Nexus Sprint Planning meeting, the Product Owner discusses a goal for the Sprint. This is called the Nexus Goal. It is the sum of all the work and Sprint Goals of the individual Scrum Teams within the Nexus. The Nexus should demonstrate the functionality that it developed to achieve the Nexus Goal at the Nexus Sprint Review.

Nexus Sprint Backlog

The Nexus Sprint Backlog contains the PBIs that have cross-team dependencies or potential integration issues. It does not contain PBIs that have no dependencies, nor does it contain tasks from the individual Scrum Team Sprint Backlogs. It is used to highlight dependencies and the flow of work during the Sprint. It is updated at least daily, often as part of the Nexus Daily Scrum.

Integrated Increment

The Integrated Increment is the integrated aggregation of all work completed by *all* the Scrum Teams in a Nexus. The Integrated Increment must be usable and potentially releasable, which means it must meet the definition of "Done" agreed to by the Development Team. The Product Owner is a key stakeholder for it and defines the quality criteria that the Product Increment must meet. The Integrated Increment is inspected at the Nexus Sprint Review.

Artifact Transparency

Just like Scrum, on which it builds, Nexus is based on transparency. The NIT works with the Scrum Teams in the Nexus, and the broader organization, to ensure that all Scrum and Nexus artifacts are visible and that the state of the Integrated Increment can be easily understood.

Decisions made based on the state of Nexus artifacts are only as effective as the level of artifact transparency. Incomplete or partial information will lead to incorrect or flawed decisions, making it difficult or impossible to guide the Nexus effectively to minimize risk and maximize value.

The greatest challenge a Nexus faces is detecting and resolving dependencies before technical debt accumulates to an unacceptable level. The test of unacceptable technical debt is when the Nexus tries to integrate the work from its Scrum Teams. When that integration fails, the unresolved dependencies remain hidden in the code and test base, lowering or negating the value of the software.

DEFINITION OF "DONE" IN NEXUS

The NIT is responsible for a definition of "Done" that can be applied to the Integrated Increment developed each Sprint. All Scrum Teams of a Nexus adhere to this definition of "Done."

The Increment is done only when it has been determined to be usable and potentially releasable by the Product Owner. A PBI can be considered done when that functionality has been successfully added to the product and integrated into the Increment.

All Scrum Teams are responsible for developing and integrating their work into an Increment that satisfies these attributes. Individual Scrum Teams may choose to apply a more stringent definition of "Done" within their own teams, but they cannot apply less rigorous criteria than agreed for the Increment.

WHAT DO YOU NEED TO GET STARTED WITH NEXUS?

Nexus is based on the Scrum Framework and adds minimal events, roles, and artifacts to increase transparency, communication, and collaboration among teams. The new Nexus events, roles, and artifacts help ensure a successfully Integrated Increment is developed. Just like with Scrum, you don't need much to get started with Nexus. And just like with Scrum, Nexus is simple to learn but hard to master. Here are the minimal but required prerequisites you will need to implement Nexus.

You should have

✓ Scrum experience.

✓ A single Product Backlog, and a single Product Owner, for a single Product.

✓ Identified teams that will be in a Nexus. They should have an overview of the Nexus Framework.

✓ Identified members who will make up the NIT for the Nexus.

✓ A definition of "Done."

✓ Identified Sprint cadence.

CLOSING

Nexus is simple to understand, but mastering it takes practice and feedback. Like Scrum, its basic concepts are simple. Like Scrum, it is also not prescriptive; it says that you need to engage the Nexus in planning the Sprint, but it does not tell you how to do that because there are many techniques that you might find useful to help you to plan. In the following chapters, we will explore applying Nexus in a case study. In doing so, we will often illustrate how Nexus works by using specific complementary practices. These are not specifically part of Nexus, but they will help you understand better how Nexus works. With that, let's get started with what it takes to form a Nexus in Chapter 3.

FORMING 3 A NEXUS

Now, with a basic understanding of Nexus established, we can focus on how an organization would apply Nexus to deliver a product. To provide a rich canvas for illustration, we have chosen a consumer product with hardware, embedded software, and mobile and web interfaces. Eventually, we will illustrate team distribution and multi-vendor interactions.

As we follow this fictional team on its journey, you may react as one of our colleagues did: "These teams make all the typical mistakes!" We have them do that for a reason, because you may make these same mistakes. We want to show something important—that you can make mistakes and still recover, and that the only way you will succeed is to inspect and adapt not only the product that you are building, but also the way that you are working.

And so we begin at the point where you will most likely begin, with the formation of a team.

A small startup feels that they have a great opportunity in home security systems. They have a product prototype, a doorbell equipped with a wireless webcam, as well as a motion sensor–equipped cameras that can be positioned anywhere around the periphery of a building so long as they are within Wi-Fi range, with the ability to receive mobile alerts and view cameras from mobile devices. It tested well in focus groups, and the company has received a first round of venture funding.

While the prototype was built with a single team, they know that they can't make the progress they need without more people—they need to scale. Everyone on the team has experience using Scrum, having worked on several successful products already. Compared to what they've built before, the webcam is really like many products: the camera/motion sensor involves developing hardware and embedded software that can be updated over the air. The mobile application must be developed and optimized for at least iOS and Android, and they need a way to keep the software updated with new features and security updates.

They decide to form teams around the components of the solution: one team for the device, one team for mobile development, and one for parts of the solution that will run in the cloud. They also decide that they will work in two-week Sprints, as they had been doing when they developed the prototype.

This example illustrates a typical way to form teams—around areas of specialized knowledge needed to develop specific components. While this is a very common way to organize, it's not the only way—nor is it the best way, as we shall see; large products can have many other aspects that might provide ways to organize teams, including platforms and technology stacks, geographical location, personas and features, and components.

The best strategy is the one that lets each team work relatively independently, in parallel, while continuously integrating their work. To do this, the teams need to align three different forces that create or eliminate cross-team dependencies, depending on their decisions.

1. **The team structure.** When teams are self-contained and cross-functional, they don't have to depend on others to get work done.
2. **The work structure.** When work is broken into small chunks that can be worked independently by a single team, teams also don't have to depend on others to get work done.
3. **The product architecture.** When the product is built from small, self-contained components that can be changed independently, teams don't have to depend on others to get work done.

In reality, complete team independence is never wholly possible, but working to align these forces leads to more independent teams, more easily managed work, and better, more resilient products (see Figure 3-1.)

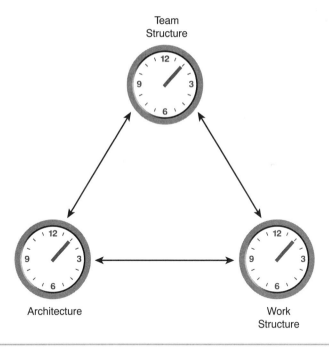

Figure 3-1 Balancing team structure, product architecture, and work composition helps organizations reduce or avoid cross-team dependencies

EVOLVING A CROSS-FUNCTIONAL TEAM

As the original product team splits into three Scrum Teams, the team members choose to uphold a central strategy for increased flexibility and improved maintainability: they want to make sure that everyone, no matter what they work on, has a broad understanding of the overall product. To do this, they decide that every couple of Sprints they will rotate people between Scrum Teams so that they eventually get to contribute to every part of the product. This will also allow them to, eventually, evolve from their current component-specialist teams into more flexible cross-functional teams.

They understand that this will make team formation a little more challenging, since they will have to re-form the teams when people rotate, but they feel that it will help to create a greater sense of shared purpose across all the teams and will enable them to progress faster, with greater flexibility, over time. They also feel that it would give team members a chance to learn new things and grow their skills, and that this would help increase their sense of satisfaction over time.

They also understand that their velocity may suffer somewhat in the short run because many of the team members will be learning new skills and technologies. They decide to work toward cross-functional teams anyway because it will reduce their inter-team dependencies and improve the overall flow and balance of work between teams.

The ideal situation is for any team to be able to work on any Product Backlog item. Within each team, it's also ideal if any team member can do any kind of work. Most teams in most organizations are pretty far from this ideal, but it's still a worthy goal. The more specialized people's skills, the more difficult it is to have a smooth flow of work.

There are always good reasons why this isn't possible. If a team is building a control system for an aircraft, not everyone on the team needs to be an aeronautical engineer—but it's good if someone is. However, if all team members are specialized, then there will be Sprints in which some, or maybe even many, of the team members can't help with the work. Velocity will take a big hit.

Scrum Teams function best when everyone has deep skills in at least one or a couple of areas, has a broad base of common skills, and is working to improve their skills in areas where the team is currently weak. Everyone should have broad business knowledge, and empathy for, if not understanding of, customers.

In cases where certain deep technical skills are scarce, pairing developers provides a way to share knowledge. Where teams themselves have specialties, rotating team members between teams helps to broaden the base of technical and even business domain knowledge.

PRACTICE: OPENING THE CODE BASE

The teams decide early on to open the code base to anyone on any of the teams. This supports their desire to spread knowledge of the code across the whole team by rotating members between teams and developing "T-shaped" skills.

To ensure that code quality remains high, they put a couple of practices in place: first, they build and test every code check-in using continuous integration. Next, they use trunk-based development practices to detect changes that would introduce defects into the code base.

To do this means that every application program interface (API) has to have unit tests, and automated regression tests are needed to make sure that completed work is not broken by a change. The teams also decide from the beginning that APIs will never be changed but will be versioned; "changes" will require publishing a new API and then collaborating with users of the old API to get them to migrate to the new API. When an API is no longer used, it can be removed.

Opening the code base to modification by anyone on the team enables the flexibility that teams need to be effective, but there's more to consider than just a security access issue. To make it work requires teams to bring together several related practices.

- **Trunk-based development.** There is one official, single source of truth in the code. No feature branches. No private branches. Everyone works off the same repository and commits to the same repository.[1]

- **Continuous integration.** Every change that a developer commits to the source repository must be built and subjected to a set of tests that evaluate whether the code meets agreed-upon quality standards.

- **Automated API-based testing.** Everything needs to have an API, and every API must have a robust set of unit tests that ensure that the API hasn't been broken.

- **Versioned API management.** APIs never change. New APIs are created, existing clients migrate to new APIs when they are ready, and unused APIs are removed when clients are no longer using them. This prevents API changes from breaking code and from introducing enforced "catch-up" periods when code may be broken until everyone converts to the new API.

- **Code review.** Pair programming (which is a kind of continuous code review), or periodic code review supported by automated code review built into the continuous integration process, provides developers with frequent feedback that helps them improve the quality of their work. Opening the code base requires every developer to practice very high levels of code hygiene; lapses quickly create problems that affect the entire team. Code review practices also help the team collaborate and share information more effectively.

We'll talk more about these practices and how they help teams scale Scrum in Chapter 7, "The Nexus in Emergency Mode."

PRACTICE: FORM TEAMS AROUND INCREMENTS OF BUSINESS VALUE

The teams in the case study have organized around platforms and technologies, at least for now. This was a natural division for them based on the specialty areas of knowledge they needed to develop the necessary parts of their product. When large products are developed using a single set of platforms or technologies, teams need a different way to partition

---

1. For more information about trunk-based development, see https://trunkbaseddevelopment.com/.

themselves. One approach is to use techniques that have emerged from User-Centered Design like *Personas* and *outcomes* or, alternately, Value Areas, to partition teams.[2]

A *persona* is a description of a particular type of user of the Product.[3] When used to partition teams, the important information about the persona are the outcomes the persona wants to achieve. When splitting work between teams, focusing a team on a particular persona and all its outcomes is useful because it will force the team to learn more about that persona and its desired outcomes.[4]

Depending on its capacity, a team can take on more than one persona. If a persona has too many outcomes for a single team to deliver, different teams can deliver different outcomes for a single persona.

Value Areas are a similar concept to the persona-outcome concept.[5] Using personas and outcomes aligns better with the way User Experience professionals often talk about user needs, whereas the concept of Value Areas is more general. Either approach can yield the desired teaming result: well-formed teams with a well-reasoned scope of responsibilities.

Another way to engage a team and align it with delivering business value is to let it own a key measure that influences business performance, and set goals accordingly. Example measures include an app store rating, a net promoter score, or some measure of customer retention like repeat sales, frequency of app usage, or follow-on sales within a particular time period. Giving teams something they can own and improve helps them stay focused and motivated.

2. Another technique that is useful for breaking down product capabilities into smaller units, Impact Mapping, is discussed in Chapter 4, "Planning in Nexus." Teams can be organized around Actors or Impacts.
3. http://www.uiaccess.com/accessucd/personas.html
4. Tony Ulwick's book *What Customers Want* is written from a consumer products perspective, but it contains many insights into the challenge of defining products based on a "jobs to be done" model.
5. https://sites.google.com/a/scrumplop.org/published-patterns/value-stream/value-areas.

PRACTICE: FORM SELF-ORGANIZING TEAMS

The teams decide to practice self-organization from the start, and they start with how they will form teams in the Nexus. They resist assigning people to teams based on team member experience and expertise because they want to promote flexibility and emphasize openness and willingness to experiment to learn new things. Forming teams is the most basic decision they have to make, and they want people to choose the team on which they work to let team members explore new areas of interest if they so choose. They also want to encourage commitment of the team members to their teams and to one another.

The typical project management approach treats people like interchangeable cogs in a machine, but the reality is that everyone has different strengths, weaknesses, goals, and aspirations. Letting people choose who they work with sends them a powerful message that they are trusted to make good decisions. This is a big first step toward enabling that team to come together to achieve something really remarkable.

Beyond just choosing their own membership, teams need to come to agreement on their code of conduct, what they value, and how they will work with each other.[6] Even when team members have worked together before, letting them self-organize can signal that they need to reset old behaviors, especially when new members are joining the team.

Contrast this with the situation in which a manager assigns team members to a team. They may or may not want to work together, and whether they do or not, it will be hard for them to feel mutually accountable for results. If the team dynamics don't work, it's the manager's problem to fix them. If they can't control something as basic as team membership, they aren't really empowered and will struggle to collaborate effectively.

---

6. Commitment is one of the five values of Scrum; the others are focus, openness, respect, and courage. For a deeper perspective, watch Ken Schwaber and Jeff Sutherland discuss the importance of Scrum Values in the webcast at https://www.scrum.org/About/All-Articles/articleType/ArticleView/articleId/1020/Changes-to-the-Scrum-Guide--ScrumPulse-Episode-14, and download the latest Scrum Guide at http://www.scrumguides.org.

GROWING A NEXUS

All of the current team members have worked together before, and they know the risks of adding too many people too quickly. They've had good experiences with using pairing techniques to add new people to the team, and they plan to use it again now, at least for bringing new people on board. Since they feel that they already have good working relationships, they want to keep to a lightweight, informal Scrum-of-Scrums approach to cross-team coordination.[7]

Because they plan to grow their teams quickly, they decide to have a Scrum Master on each team. The Scrum Masters will also develop, but they will adjust their work commitments to put their Scrum Master responsibilities first. These Scrum Masters will also act as representatives of the individual teams and attend the Scrum of Scrums to discuss progress and impediments at the team level.

This is where many organizations start—with a single Scrum Team that needs to grow into several teams. Often, team members who are experienced with Scrum find that a Scrum-of-Scrums approach feels familiar and comfortable.

STARTING SMALL AND THEN GROWING

The biggest advantage to scaling slowly is that it allows the organization to limit risk and validate assumptions of whether it can meet its goals with its current knowledge and capabilities. Another advantage is that growing teams slowly reduces complexity by limiting the number of people involved and reducing cross-team dependencies. With fewer teams,

---

7. The "Scrum of Scrums" approach is "a technique to scale Scrum up to large groups (over a dozen people), consisting of dividing the groups into Agile teams of 5–10. Each daily scrum within a sub-team ends by designating one member as 'ambassador' to participate in a daily meeting with ambassadors from other teams, called the Scrum of Scrums.... The Scrum of Scrums proceeds otherwise as a normal daily meeting, with ambassadors reporting completions, next steps and impediments on behalf of the teams they represent. Resolution of impediments is expected to focus on the challenges of coordination between the teams; solutions may entail agreeing to interfaces between teams, negotiating responsibility boundaries, etc." Source: https://www.agilealliance.org/glossary/scrum-of-scrums, and https://www.scrum.org/Blog/ArtMID/1765/ArticleID/12/Resurrecting-the-Much-Maligned-Scrum-of-Scrums.

teams can better collaborate. Starting small means starting slow and accepting that productivity will take a hit as new team members join the team.

Starting with all teams at once involves everyone in the beginning, but is more risky, inefficient, and costly. The question "Could we have done the same or more with less?" always lingers. Productivity may also be reduced in a big bang start because it takes time to address integration, consistency, and cultural issues.

USING PAIRING AND "INTERNSHIP" TO GROW SCRUM TEAMS

> *They also decide that the teams themselves will interview all new team members; no managers will hire outside the team, and new team members must be unanimously accepted by their fellow team members.*

Rotating new people through existing high-performing teams helps to extend the culture and cohesion of the existing teams, if done correctly. It can also destabilize the team and drain productivity if new team members are added too quickly. Many organizations have found that pairing new hires with experienced team members for at least a couple of Sprints helps them learn the code as well as becoming steeped in the team's culture.

One way this kind of pairing and rotation can be used is the "internship" model in which one or more new team members are added to existing teams, for a period of time, to learn about the product, the code, and the culture. When ready, these new team members will leave the existing teams to form a new team, leaving the original teams intact and potentially ready to accept new "interns" (see Figure 3-2).

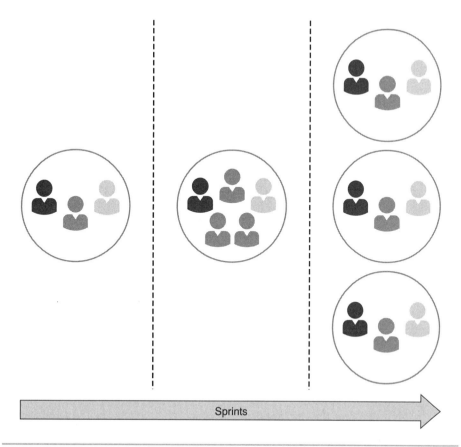

Figure 3-2 New team members are added to existing teams to learn team culture and values. As teams grow large enough, they split into separate teams who can then continue to grow.

WHY ONLY THREE TO NINE SCRUM TEAMS IN A NEXUS?

There isn't much coordination overhead when two Scrum Teams need to work together. The two teams can work out, between themselves, who does what without much formalization or structure. They can just talk.

The upper limit of nine teams in a Nexus is more of a practical matter than an absolute limit. Just as the effectiveness of a Scrum Team tapers off and declines due to interpersonal communication overhead as its size grows beyond nine members, a Nexus suffers from the same effects—intra-team and inter-team cohesion begin to fragment and splinter, and the people in the Nexus find it harder to effectively self-organize.

FORMING THE NEXUS INTEGRATION TEAM

> *During their third Sprint Retrospective, the teams raise some problems. First, they have a separate Product Backlog for each team, and it is starting to feel like they are producing three separate Products, not one. The Product Owner is feeling overwhelmed and challenged to spend enough time guiding each team.*
>
> *As a possible solution, she suggests adding two more Product Owners to be able to handle all the work of prioritizing the Backlogs and working with the teams. She feels that the separate Product Backlogs have started to drift from the original product goals, and she doesn't have the time to keep all three in sync. The other team members understand her frustration at not being able to be everywhere at once, but everyone agrees that adding Product Owners will only exacerbate the "three Products" problem.*
>
> *In addition, despite a strong, cohesive core of team members who had worked together, the teams don't feel that the teams are working together very well now. They work fine within their own teams and on their own backlogs but had major integration issues at the end of this last Sprint.*
>
> *An informal "integration team" of the most senior members of the teams has formed, and they are jumping in and solving problems for the teams rather than helping the teams to solve the problems themselves. They are being pulled into all the separate Daily Scrums in addition to the Scrum of Scrums with the Scrum Masters. It is turning into the very kind of centralized control mechanism that nobody wants.*
>
> *Team members are getting frustrated that they were not able to easily integrate work from all the teams, and no team is taking any accountability for the integration issues. It's always "the other team's fault." What they thought would be easy was turning out to be very hard.*

The challenges the case study's teams face are typical: how to uphold a single consistent product vision, and to build a single integrated product, while working as separate teams. When teams encounter these challenges, their history with top-down centralized control approaches sometimes creates a pull that is too hard to resist.

Nexus introduces a Nexus Integration Team (NIT) to help teams deal with these challenges. Despite its name, the NIT isn't usually a standing team with full-time team members, nor is it actually responsible for integration, although it *is* accountable for integration. It only works on Product Backlog Items in the case of emergencies when things have gone horribly wrong and someone needs to stabilize the situation. Instead, it is usually a virtual team composed of members from the Scrum Teams themselves, plus the Product Owner (see Figure 3-3).

The NIT's role is much like that of a Scrum Master on a Scrum Team—it provides a mechanism to identify issues and facilitate solutions, but it does not take over and solve problems for the Scrum Teams. The difference from the very informal nature of the Scrum-of-Scrums approach initially used by the teams in the case study is that the NIT has very specific accountabilities and resulting responsibilities for which there are certain proven practices that help it fulfill those responsibilities. Membership can vary over time depending on the impediments the Nexus experiences.

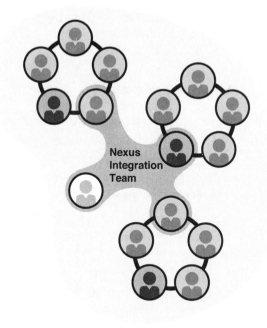

Figure 3-3 The NIT is composed of members of the Scrum Teams plus the Product Owner

The NIT is *accountable* for a releasable integrated Product being delivered at least once at the end of every Sprint. That confuses some people, and they think that it actually pulls the bits together and integrates them. This is precisely what it does *not* do. The Scrum Teams are still *responsible* for producing working software. Being *accountable* means that the NIT provides focus and helps the Scrum Teams resolve issues when they cannot deliver an integrated, working increment, in much the same way a Scrum Master coaches the Development Team to resolve their own impediments.[8]

WHO IS ON THE NEXUS INTEGRATION TEAM?

The only mandatory member of the NIT is the Product Owner. The other members are usually the member of their Scrum Team with the deepest and broadest technical skills and good coaching skills. This person may also be the Scrum Master for the team, but it is a mistaken belief that the NIT must be wholly composed of Scrum Masters. The NIT has to provide technical leadership as well as Scrum leadership, and it sometimes needs to help resolve deep technical or architectural issues. Team members with only Scrum Master skills can't always do this.

HOW DOES A NEXUS WORK?

As you will see in subsequent chapters, the structure of the Nexus and the composition of its teams will change over time as needs change and the skills of team members improve. What we have described here is a reasonable, and fairly realistic, starting point. The team structure is not perfect, but the team members believe that it will be good enough to get work done and to improve.

With the Nexus formed, we can now turn our attention to how the teams will work together to produce an integrated Product Increment. In Chapter 4, we'll take a closer look at how the teams come together to refine the Product Backlog, resolve dependencies, and plan a Sprint.

---

8. The main difference between responsibility and accountability is that responsibility can be shared whereas accountability cannot. Being accountable not only means being responsible for something but also ultimately being answerable for your actions. For more explanation, see http://www.diffen.com/difference/Accountability_vs_Responsibility.

PLANNING 4 IN NEXUS

Coordinating work across multiple Scrum Teams can be confusing and chaotic without a systematic planning approach, as the team quickly discovered. When more than one team works on a Product Backlog, the overhead of coordinating between teams can grow until it dramatically slows progress. A Nexus uses a variety of practices to reduce complexity and the overhead of coordinating multi-team development.

CONSOLIDATING AND VALIDATING THE PRODUCT BACKLOG

The Scrum Teams come together with the Product Owner to consolidate their separate work into a single prioritized Product Backlog. This takes a bit of effort, since they've gone a little off track in each of their separate backlogs, adding features that made sense in isolation but don't fit together when the product is considered as a whole. As the Product Owner orders the backlog, she and the teams validate that the backlog items have not drifted from the original product goal. The Product Owner uses impact mapping, a useful practice to see whether they are working on the PBIs that will add the most value. With the teams, she creates the Impact Map with the teams shown in Figure 4-1.[1]

---

1. For more information about Impact Mapping, see Gojko Adzic's website at https://www.impactmapping.org.

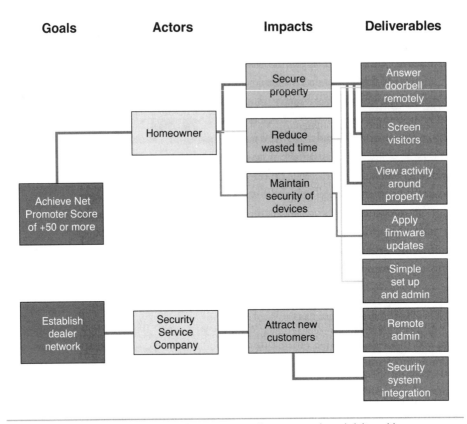

Figure 4-1 An Impact Map showing the connection between goals and deliverables

In Figure 4-1, the lines connecting *impacts* with *deliverables* illustrate that more than one deliverable may need to be delivered to achieve a desired impact; for example, to achieve the impact *Secure property*, the user of the product will need to be able to answer the doorbell remotely, screen visitors, and view activity around the property.

Validating the Product Backlog Items (PBIs) against business objectives helps to make sure that nothing goes missing in the consolidation process, and that nothing extra has crept in while the teams were working separately.

All Product Owners face the risk that their Product Backlog becomes filled with items that have no connection back to the product's original business goals. An Impact Map helps them avoid this by visualizing the scope of a product. It focuses on four aspects.

- **The Goals.** The root of an Impact Map answers the most important question: Why are we doing this? In the case of our team, they need to have a successful initial product launch, which for their venture capitalist funders means achieving a Net Promoter Score of +50 or better.[2] They also need to sign up at least one dealer, typically a security services company.

- **The Actors.** The actors answer the following questions: Who can produce the desired effect? Who can obstruct it? Who are the consumers or users of our product? Who will be impacted by it? These are the **actors** whom the solution will need to support.

- **The Impacts.** The impacts describe the desired outcomes of the actors in the context of our business goal. It answers the following questions: What does our solution need to do for the actors? What things do we need to help them achieve? These are the impacts that we're trying to create.

- **The Deliverables.** The deliverables answer the following questions: What can we do, as an organization or a delivery team, to support the required impacts? What is the solution going to do for the actors to help them achieve their desired outcomes? These are the deliverables, software features, and organizational activities that our solution will need to provide. These will become, or map to, high-level PBIs.

Product Owners should embrace and represent the product vision they've created with stakeholders. They can use a variety of different techniques, ranging from the simple ones, like elevator pitches, to more comprehensive techniques like opportunity canvases.[3] When the Product Owner and the rest of the team lose sight of product goals, the Product Backlog can become bloated with excess features that distract and divert teams from achieving their business objectives. This is a particular problem in larger organizations with many stakeholders, where teams can be challenged to prevent pet features and ideas from creeping into the Product Backlog. Impact Mapping is a good way for everyone in a Nexus to understand and validate the value of their work toward business goals.

---

2. For more information about Net Promoter Scores, see https://www.netpromoter.com/know/.

3. For more information about the opportunity canvas technique, see http://jpattonassociates.com/opportunity-canvas/.

REFINING THE PRODUCT BACKLOG[4]

> As the Scrum Teams and the Product Owner look at the Impact Map, some questions arise. Some PBIs look like duplicates, having come from different Scrum Team backlogs, so they combine the ones that overlap. In other cases they have PBIs that don't tie back to impacts, so these get dropped, and there seem to be some impacts with no PBIs, so these get created. The Product Owner orders the resulting list, and they all feel that they have a much clearer picture of what they should work on.
>
> Or so they think. As the teams talk through who will work on what, they quickly realize that they have a problem: Virtually all the new, combined PBIs cross all the teams (see Figure 4-2). They can see what they need to do to create a complete product, but they're not yet at the point where any of the teams can pull work from the Product Backlog.

Product Backlog Items	Device Team	Mobile Team	Web/Services Team
1 – Respond to doorbell using mobile or web device	✔	✔	✔
2 – View selected security camera over web or mobile device	✔	✔	✔
3 – Alert mobile device or web client that doorbell has rung	✔	✔	✔
4 – Alert mobile device or web client that motion was detected	✔	✔	✔
5 – Alert more than one mobile device or web client		✔	✔
6 – Alert mobile device or web client that sensor battery is low	✔	✔	✔
7 – Turn off/on alerts for a mobile or web client		✔	✔
8 – Update device firmware	✔		
9 – Set up/admin device from web or mobile phone	✔	✔	✔
10 – Remote device admin API	✔		
11 – Integrate with external security systems	✔		

Figure 4-2 The initial Product Backlog, prior to Product Backlog Refinement, showing team dependencies

---

4. Refining the Product Backlog can be done by the Nexus at any time, not just while planning a Sprint. Since it is a natural precursor to Sprint Planning, we present it here as if it was part of the Sprint Planning process.

What the Nexus begins to realize is that many of the items in the Product Backlog have dependencies that make developing them a complex multi-team effort. They need to break the backlog items down into separate items that a single team can work on, but they also need to do this in a way that will produce a single integrated product at least by the end of the Sprint, if not more frequently. If they don't, they will almost be back to where they started with all separate and unintegrated work.

CROSS-TEAM PRODUCT BACKLOG REFINEMENT

The Product Owner and the rest of the Nexus get together to refine the Product Backlog, breaking down the large backlog items just enough to minimize the team dependencies. They do this as a large group exercise to make sure they have all the information they need to refine the backlog items. For some items, this means a small group goes off in a corner to discuss how they might do this. In fact, they find that using Open Space principles helps them self-organize the work.[5]

The teams in the Nexus continually refine the Product Backlog with the Product Owner as needed throughout the Sprint, whenever they find backlog items that will require too much effort for one team to deliver in a Sprint. This is similar to the refinement that teams do in Scrum, adding detail, estimates, and order to items in the Product Backlog.[6] In Nexus, Refinement also means breaking down PBIs to minimize cross-team dependencies.

There is no specific time box for Refinement, nor is there a specific time during the Sprint when teams work on Refinement. The outcome of Refinement is a backlog item that is "Ready," which means that everyone agrees that they understand it well enough to include it in a Sprint. In the context of Nexus, "Ready" includes identifying and minimizing dependencies so that, as much as possible, a single team can work on the PBI.

---

5. For more information about applying Open Space practices to running meetings, see http://openspaceworld.org/wp2/.

6. http://www.scrumguides.org/scrum-guide.html#artifacts-productbacklog

Refinement is frequently a precursor to Sprint Planning, and it may happen when teams find implicit dependencies between backlog items. To do this effectively, the teams need to look a little ahead to anticipate the work that might need to be done first to free the constraints for future work. The amount of time will vary from Nexus to Nexus, depending on the number and complexity of dependencies. A Nexus with a long string of dependencies will need to look further ahead than one with simple unitary dependencies. The case study teams have chosen to look three Sprints ahead at first, but there is no strict rule, and the amount of foresight will even vary over time.

This anticipatory view doesn't limit the Nexus from releasing as frequently as they need to; they can release continuously if they have something of value to deliver, but it does help them detect possible cross-team collaboration problems before they actually cause problems.

During Refinement, the Nexus does just enough analysis to understand, detect, and minimize the cross-team dependencies. This usually results in backlog items that are "thinly sliced".[7] The teams know that they have sufficiently refined the PBIs when a Scrum Team can develop them without conflict with other Scrum Teams. The key to this is "anticipation"—having enough insight into the backlog items to ensure that any integration issues are exposed so that the teams can work on them.

> While they refine the Product Backlog, the teams are also capturing the dependencies between PBIs, so that they know how the teams will need to sequence their work.
>
> The original PBI # 1, "Respond to doorbell using mobile or web device," has been split into two large items: one that deals with the simple act of ringing the doorbell, and one that deals with conversing with a visitor through the built-in microphone/speaker (implementing a simple intercom). The reason for this is that the product should be able to work as a doorbell button, albeit a very expensive one, even if nothing else works.

---

7. For more information on slicing PBIs to reduce their size and complexity so that they fit in a single Sprint, or to reduce cross-team dependencies, see Barry Overeem's excellent blog on story slicing at http://www.barryovereem.com/the-story-slicing-workshop/.

All team members work together to refine the PBIs so that they are small enough to be accomplished by one team in a single Sprint. The Product Owner also orders these new backlog items. The results of their Product Backlog Refinement are shown in Figure 4-3.

Product Backlog Items	Device Team	Mobile Team	Web/Services Team
1 – Alert user(s) that doorbell has been rung			
1.1 – Create alerting service			✔
10 – Set up/admin device from web or mobile phone			
10.1 – Remote device set-up/admin API	✔		
9 – Update device firmware	✔		
5 – Generate #motionDetected alert	✔		
1 – Alert user(s) that doorbell has been rung			
1.2 – Respond to button press (ring bell, raise #doorbellRung alert)	✔		
1.3 – Detect #doorbellRung alert event, notify mobile user		✔	
2 – Conduct conversation with visitor through doorbell speaker			
2.1 – Conduct 2-way voice conversation via universal client API	✔		
2.2 – Conduct 2-way voice conversation via universal client API on mobile device		✔	
3 – View selected security camera over web or mobile device			
3.1 – Stream video using standard opensource API	✔		
3.2 – Display streaming video on mobile device using standard opensource API		✔	
3.3 – Display streaming video in web browser using standard opensource API			✔
6 – Alert more than one mobile device or web client			✔
7 – Generate #sensorBatteryLow event	✔		
8 – Turn off/on alerts for a mobile or web client			
8.1 – Turn off/on alerts for mobile client		✔	
8.2 – Turn off/on alerts for web client			✔
10 – Set up/admin device from web or mobile phone			
10.2 – Set up/admin device from mobile phone		✔	
10.3 – Set up/admin device from web			✔
11 – Integrate with external security systems			✔
1 – Alert user(s) that doorbell has been rung			
1.4 – Detect #doorbellRung alert event, notify web user			✔
2 – Conduct conversation with visitor through doorbell speaker			
2.3 – Conduct 2-way voice conversation via universal client API in web browser session			✔

Figure 4-3 Refined and ordered Product Backlog

PRODUCT BACKLOG ITEM DEPENDENCIES

> *The Product Owner and members from the Scrum Teams with knowledge of the PBIs with cross-team dependencies meet together to break down the large, cross-team PBIs into smaller backlog items that the team can complete independently. Most of their dependencies are related to the different skills that the team members have, so in the short term there isn't any way to eliminate these.*
>
> *The biggest dependency is that the Device Team has to be involved in every backlog item because nearly everything the Mobile and Web/Services Teams need to do requires at least an API from the Device Team.*
>
> *They talk, briefly, of stepping back to define all the APIs the Mobile and Web/Services Teams will need, but they quickly realize that they don't know enough of what those teams will need to define the APIs; they will need to co-create the APIs. But first they need to break down the PBIs into smaller chunks so that the teams can work more independently.*

Different PBIs may have many different kinds of dependencies, including the following.

- **People dependencies.** Often, dependencies arise around specific people because of their specific skill or knowledge. As a result, work becomes constrained by that person's availability. For example, a team may be dependent on a particular person who may be the only one with the mathematics background to work on specific algorithms.

- **Domain expertise.** Developing solutions for different business domains can require very different skills; developing medical case management applications is very different from developing financial trading applications, which is very different from developing insurance underwriting applications. The more Development Team members know about the business domain, the more effective they will be. The Product Owner cannot be the sole source of business domain knowledge; Development Teams need it, too.

- **Technical expertise.** Backlog items related to the doorbell, camera, and motion sensors require expertise developing hardware and real-time/embedded software, as well as processing asynchronous events. Developing for different target platforms requires knowledge of different languages, platforms, and technology stack. While cross-platform tools exist, they don't always provide the flexibility to exploit platform-specific behavior or look and feel.

- **Organizational authority.** Sometimes only certain developers are permitted to touch certain parts of the code because of security or privacy concerns. This is an extreme example of domain expertise constraints. For example, a team may be dependent on a specific person who is the only one with security clearance to work on a particular component or a particular portion of the code.

- **Architectural dependencies.** Sometimes organizations enforce usage of specific components to perform specific functions, and when they do they generally have component teams that develop and evolve these components.

- **External dependencies.** Most organizations use external components and services, whether produced by commercial enterprises or open-source projects. External dependencies are the most risky and the hardest to work around, since teams have little or no control over those external organizations.

Whatever the dependency source, the teams need to split PBIs in a way that the dependencies are minimized, then sequence the backlog items as they plan to resolve or reduce the dependencies over time.

OPTIONAL PRACTICE: USING STORY MAPPING TO UNDERSTAND CAPABILITIES AND DEPENDENCIES

The Product Owner feels that the Nexus still doesn't have a good handle on what they need for the first release to get the feedback that they need. She decides that she wants to use a technique called Story Mapping to visualize how PBIs will help product users achieve their goals. It's also useful to help map out releases, which helps teams plan their Sprints.[8] The Product Owner and the teams in the Nexus work together to produce the Story Map shown in Figure 4-4.

It confirms that their current Product Backlog will give them the minimal functionality they need to launch the product in limited trials, at least for

---

8. To learn more about Jeff Patton's Story Mapping approach, see http://jpattonassociates.com/wp-content/uploads/2015/03/story_mapping.pdf.

> *Homeowners. It also highlights what they've known intuitively for a while: They don't yet know very much about what Security Services firms will need to make the product successful in the distributor channel. They will need to find a partner to help them understand this market better.*

User Story Mapping is a technique created by Jeff Patton to help teams understand how people use a product to achieve a desired outcome.[9] Figure 4-4 illustrates how a Story Map can be used to provide a narrative to the Product Backlog. As the Product Backlog grows, it is easy for teams to lose track of their original goals. Story Maps put the PBIs into context so that everyone can see the purpose behind the work. It also helps teams group related PBIs so that they can see the business implications of their planning decisions.

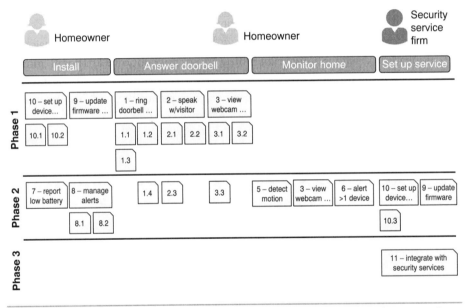

Figure 4-4 Story Maps can help teams to understand how a product will satisfy user needs over time. Story Maps also help the teams to tell the story of the product and to plan ahead.

---

9. For information about user Story Mapping, see http://jpattonassociates.com/user-story-mapping/.

In this example, the Nexus has mapped out their product delivery in three distinct phases. Within each phase, they may have many releases (they may, in fact, release some capabilities continuously), but the phases let them break out the capabilities of the product in a way that can help them make future investment decisions; for example, they may decide that Phase 3 isn't really essential to the product's success and may drop it to focus on other things.

OPTIONAL PRACTICE: USING A CROSS-TEAM REFINEMENT BOARD TO UNDERSTAND DEPENDENCIES

It's not always easy for the teams to spot dependencies, especially as the Product Backlog grows in size. The Story Map has given the Nexus insight into what is most valuable to customers, but they need to do some additional work before the Scrum Teams will be able to know what they should work on. As their Refinement proceeds, they find that simple dependency notation isn't sufficient to help them understand the cross-team dependencies.

For the Nexus to easily see the relationships between its work and to minimize cross-team dependencies, it uses a Cross-Team Refinement Board to visualize its work by teams and across Sprints (see Figure 4-5).

Dependency arrows are a way to highlight relationships of work. More arrows indicate high risk due to the number of dependent items impacted. This visualization helps the teams within the Nexus identify the "critical path"

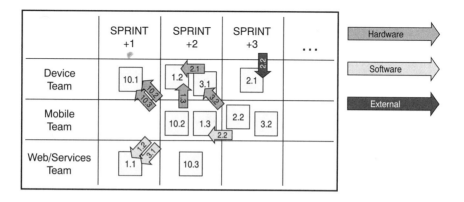

Figure 4-5 Visualizing dependencies using a Cross-Team Refinement Board

of work throughout the upcoming Sprints and provides the basis for conversations about ways to remove or minimize the impact of these dependencies.[10]

A few conventions help to convey dependency information include the following.

- **Horizontal arrows** indicate dependencies between PBIs within the same team.
- **Angled arrows** indicate dependencies between items in separate teams and in separate Sprints.
- **Arrows pointing to the right** (horizontal or angled) mean that there are dependencies on items to be worked on in the future—these must be eliminated.
- **Vertical arrows** indicate dependencies between items in separate teams but in the same Sprint—these are problematic and should be avoided if possible.
- **Arrows pointing to the left** (horizontal or angled) are not problematic, but they can become challenging if work gets delayed. An item with incoming dependencies will retain these dependencies as it gets delayed, and so the arrows may eventually become vertical, or even pointing to the right (to the future).

Dependencies are also categorized into three different types on the board.

- **Software dependencies** are most easily resolved by redefining work or moving it between teams or Sprints.
- **Hardware dependencies** are more challenging as the lead time for a hardware change may be several Sprints, but it is still within the power of the Nexus to resolve.
- **External dependencies**, like supplier commitments or dependencies on other parts of an organization, are the most difficult to resolve because their removal may be completely beyond the control of the Nexus.

---

10. For more information about conducting a Cross-Team Refinement workshop in a Nexus, see https://www.scrum.org/resources/cross-team-refinement-nexus.

The Scrum Teams start by pulling only work that is necessary for the first phase of the product, which they identified in the Story Map. The teams want to highlight their dependencies as best they can so they can figure out the best way to sequence their work. They use dependency arrows with the direction of the arrow showing which PBIs must be delivered before other PBIs (e.g., Item 10.1 must be delivered before Item 10.2.)

By visualizing the work and the dependencies on a board, the teams quickly identify two pieces of work that need to be completed by the Device Team and the Web/Services Team before the Nexus can progress. They decide to pull these items first and to sequence all the other work in the next two Sprints with as many dependencies up-front as possible; the directions of the dependency arrows are crucial here.

As the teams experiment with moving PBIs between the second and third Sprints on the board, the arrows help them see how that might affect other work. For instance, if the Device Team can't complete PBI 1.2 in the Sprint 2 and it shifts to the next Sprint, they will face four in-Sprint dependencies in the third Sprint instead of 1. The Nexus would really like to avoid this as they are already facing an external dependency in the third Sprint.

When the Nexus is done with Refinement, everyone notices something interesting, the Mobile Team has no work to pull in the first Sprint and the Web/Services Team has no items in the third Sprint. They consider changing the team structure to Feature Teams, but they are feeling pressure to get going and they think that once they get into future sprints the structure will work better. The Mobile Team feels that they have plenty they can do and they can just get started on the work without much risk of rework.

PLANNING A SPRINT IN A NEXUS

Now that they have a refined and ordered Product Backlog and some sense of how much work that backlog represents, the Nexus is ready to plan their next Sprint. Like the work of the Sprint itself, the planning process is iterative and requires some back-and-forth to arrive at a Nexus Sprint Backlog that works for all the teams.

Figure 4-6 provides a good overview of the process they will follow. In addition to the refined (and sized) Product Backlog and the capacity of each Scrum Team, the teams need to consider the current state of the product. Is it stable? Have issues been postponed? Have they been postponing issues and creating technical debt? The teams also need a clear focus for the Sprint; they need a Nexus Goal.

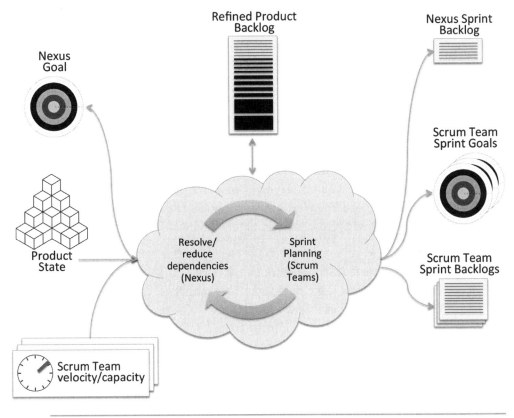

Figure 4-6 Sprint Planning in a Nexus at a glance

ESTABLISHING THE NEXUS GOAL

> *The Product Owner wants to focus on getting a working product out to a small set of customers in a test market so that she can get feedback on how they use it. While she feels confident in the general direction of the product, she has many questions for which she, personally, has no answers and is only guessing. That creates a big risk of market failure if she and the teams make the wrong call.*

The Nexus Goal is the goal for the current Sprint; if the Nexus is successful during the Sprint it achieves the Nexus Goal, and it only works on one Nexus Goal at a time. In this case, if the Nexus has a viable product to ship to target market customers in the middle of a Sprint, they should do it; there is no need to wait until the end of a Sprint to release.

ESTIMATION AND SIZING PRODUCT BACKLOG ITEMS

> *Dependencies alone often aren't sufficient for the Nexus to plan its next Sprint; it also needs to know what it can reasonably achieve. That's tough, because lately the Scrum Teams have not been very productive, and planning is always just guessing. One of the team members points out that there is even a growing #noestimates movement, so why do they need estimates anyway?[11] There is a big risk that any estimates they produce will be used by management to micro-manage the Nexus or to make inappropriate delivery commitments based on assumed velocity.*
>
> *The #noestimates discussion is lively, and everyone agrees that they don't want to have estimates used by management to track progress or set delivery expectations. Nevertheless, they need some idea of which PBIs are too large for a single team to develop in a single Sprint. These will need to be further refined before they can be worked on. The teams' goal is not to get good at predicting their velocity, but to take on only as much work in a Sprint as they can reasonably accomplish, so as not to leave work undone at the end.*

---

11. Woody Zuill gives an excellent summary of the arguments for and against #noestimates at https://vimeo.com/131194136.

The Nexus gets together and develops the relative sizing for PBIs (see Figure 4-7). They agree that this is just for them, as an aid to Sprint Planning to understand what the teams and the Nexus as a whole might accomplish. The information won't be shared outside the Nexus.

The numbers represent only relative sizing, so that a "5" is 5 times "larger" than a "1." At the upper end, a "21" merely means "really, really big," and definitely something that needs more refinement. The "5" and "8" items may also need further refinement.

In practice, not all the PBIs need to be sized, and in practice most teams would not bother to size items that they were sure they could deliver in a single Sprint. The rough sizing helps them determine how many items they could take on if they have the capacity to work on more than one. The most important thing about sizing is that it should *never* be used to set goals for teams or to compare teams; its only useful purpose is to understand whether a PBI is too large for a team to deliver in a Sprint and needs to be broken down.

1	2	3	5	8	13	21
1.2	6	9	2.1	1.1		11
1.3	8.1	10.2	2.2	10.1		
7	8.2	10.3	3.1			
1.4			3.2			
5			3.3			
			2.3			

Figure 4-7 Relative sizing helps teams gauge their capacity to complete PBIs

There is not much value in normalizing sizing estimates across teams, except in cases where it helps two teams discuss whether one team could possibly take on work that another team can't get to. Normalization driven by a desire to compare teams or to forecast productivity is usually counterproductive and leads to manipulating estimates to look better. This hurts transparency and doesn't help productivity. Managers who want to improve team productivity should focus on removing impediments that create barriers to better productivity.

OPTIONAL PRACTICE: CONNECTING PRODUCT BACKLOG ITEMS TO VALUE DELIVERY

When the Nexus must implement many PBIs in order for the customer or user to fully realize the value of the PBIs, they can group the backlog items and add information to the board depicted in Figure 4-7, as shown in Figure 4-8. The rows indicate related PBIs, and the *Outcome* describes what the Nexus expects to achieve when all the related PBIs are delivered. The *Measure* column describes what the Nexus will measure to prove its hypothesis that delivering the PBIs will result in the customer or user outcome being achieved.

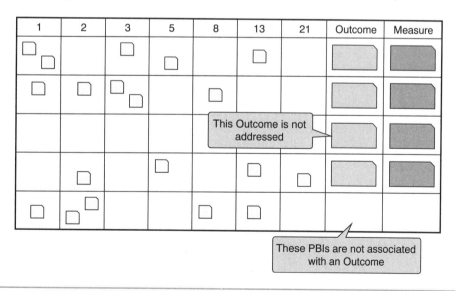

Figure 4-8 Connecting PBIs to Outcomes and Measures helps uncover gaps

This is similar to the Impact Map shown in Figure 4-1 and serves a similar purpose. The Impact Map is helpful when the Product Backlog is not yet formed, or is poorly formed, as it provides a broader view of users and business goals. Figure 4-8 is helpful once PBIs have been refined, to make sure that the team has not lost track of outcomes and to make sure that each outcome can be measured.

BUILDING THE NEXUS SPRINT BACKLOG AND SCRUM TEAM BACKLOGS

> Based on the work they have done creating the Story Map (Figure 4-4), Cross-Team Dependency Board (Figure 4-5), the refined Product Backlog (Figure 4-3), and sizing (Figure 4-7), the teams create a Nexus Sprint Backlog (see Figure 4-9). The Nexus Sprint Backlog contains just the forecasted PBIs, but not the tasks that each team will need to do to complete the PBIs. Each team estimates that they have a capacity of 10 points during the Sprint.
>
> Each Scrum Team creates its own Sprint Backlog for its own forecasted PBIs, and in those Sprint Backlogs they define the tasks that they will need to complete.

Although the NIT is *accountable* for the Nexus Sprint Backlog, the Scrum Teams actually do the work of creating the Nexus Sprint Backlog in the example here. The Nexus Sprint Backlog is an evolution of the Cross-Team Dependency Board, and some teams prefer to simply use the same board to depict both. The example Nexus Sprint Backlog shown in Figure 4-9 provides more information that helps the teams visualize the status of work during the Sprint, which helps them anticipate and respond to blocked work.

This figure is similar to the Cross-Team Dependency Board shown earlier in Figure 4-5, but this one shows the work for the current Sprint and adds

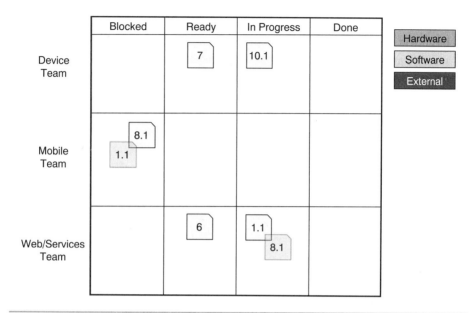

Figure 4-9 The Nexus uses the Nexus Sprint Backlog to manage the flow of work

information for the PBIs (whether they are Ready, Blocked, In Progress, or Done), and it represents cross-team dependencies as overlapping cards rather than arrows.

- A card is placed *over the bottom-left corner* of a PBI to show that it must be completed before the other item.
- An overlapping card is placed over the bottom-right corner of an item to indicate that another item is dependent on this item.

So in Figure 4-9, the Web/Services Team completing PBI 1.1 will *unblock* the ability of the Mobile Team to work on PBI 8.1. Showing items 1.1 and 8.1 are tagged as software dependencies, because one team needs an API to be developed by another team. Showing dependencies in the Nexus Sprint Backlog helps the teams easily understand the current state of cross-team dependencies.

> *What the Nexus discovers, as they plan the Sprint, is that they were right to be worried about how to divide the work between team. No matter what they do, with the current team structure, the Mobile Team doesn't have enough to do in the current Sprint. They consider changing the team structure but they feel pressure to get going, and they really aren't ready for a feature team structure as it would require every team to be able to do hardware, mobile, and web work.*
>
> *To work toward that goal, they decide that they will pair members of the mobile team with members of the device and web/services teams for the first Sprint to improve the team members' breadth and depth of knowledge of the code. After the first Sprint, they will decide how to fix the team structures.*

Now that they have a plan for the Sprint (the Nexus Sprint Backlog and the individual team Sprint Backlogs), the Nexus is ready to get started on its Sprint. The journey continues in Chapter 5, "Running a Sprint in Nexus."

How Long Does Sprint Planning Take?

The different techniques that the Nexus in the case study uses to plan its Sprint may leave some of you thinking, "Wow, that's a lot of work to plan a Sprint!" The Scrum Guide time-boxes Sprint Planning to a *maximum* of eight hours for a 1-month Sprint, with less time needed for shorter Sprints. Nexus Sprint planning should take a similar amount of time, though in reality, it takes what it takes, as it will for all the other Nexus events. If it takes a Nexus longer than a day for Nexus Sprint Planning, that is an opportunity to inspect, adapt, and improve.

The Nexus in the case study had a lot of work to do to combine multiple Product Backlogs into a single Product Backlog, and to refine the Product Backlog. Now that their Product Backlog is in good shape, they should be able to continuously refine the Product Backlog, and their Sprint Planning will be easier. The other thing that makes the first Sprint harder to plan is having to understand and visualize dependencies for several Sprints. When they plan their next Sprint they won't have to do all this work, and they can simply look one Sprint further than they did last time.

How far ahead do they need to look? That depends on the number and complexity of cross-team dependencies. Scrum Teams with few dependencies may only need to look a Sprint ahead; those with very complex dependencies may need to look a couple. The more the Scrum Teams can refine PBIs so that they are small and independent, the less they will have to anticipate future work.

CLOSING

The biggest differences between Nexus Sprint Planning and Sprint Planning in Scrum is that, in Nexus, planning must also consider cross-team dependencies. Product Backlog Refinement, which is optional in Scrum, becomes essential to making sure that the dependencies are minimized. Planning also becomes iterative, as sometimes cross-team dependencies are not evident at first.

With a plan in hand, we'll now see what challenges that plan gives rise to, as we move on to Chapter 5.

RUNNING A SPRINT IN NEXUS

The daily rhythm in a Nexus does not change much for a team that is accustomed to using Scrum. Each team still has its Daily Scrum meeting, and when they encounter issues for which they need help from other teams, they now have a Nexus Daily Scrum that helps them raise and resolve the issue(s). The Nexus produces an Integrated Increment, just as in Scrum. At the end of the Sprint they have a Nexus Sprint Review, which is for the whole Nexus. They also conduct a Sprint Retrospective for the Nexus as a whole, as well as having individual Sprint Retrospectives (see Figure 5-1).

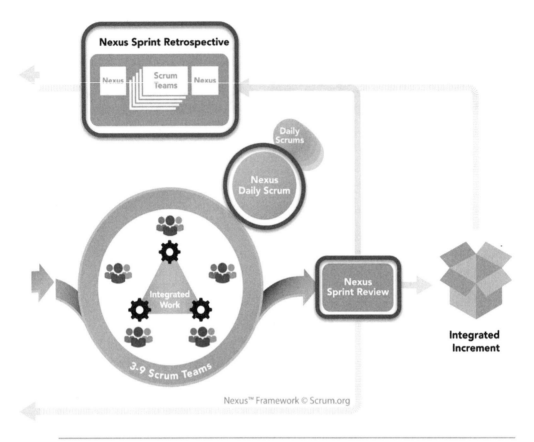

Figure 5-1 Nexus is still Scrum, it just adapts a few of the events

THE NEXUS DAILY SCRUM

On the first day after Sprint Planning, representatives from each team get together for the Nexus Daily Scrum to discuss cross-team integration issues that might block the Scrum Teams from making progress on the Nexus Goal and the items in the Nexus Sprint Backlog.

Not being sure whom to send, each team sends its Scrum Master, but they immediately discover a problem: Scrum Masters aren't the right representatives from the teams to discuss the initial integration issue they encounter, which is

> *how to establish a continuous integration process that enables them to integrate code whenever a developer delivers it.*
>
> *In the past, each team had its own build process but, as a Nexus, they have decided that this delays integration too long. The Scrum Masters attending the Nexus Daily Scrum quickly realize this and go back to their teams to get the developers who are most knowledgeable about continuous integration to attend the Nexus Daily Scrum.*

This illustrates an important point: the *right* people to attend the Nexus Daily Scrum may vary, depending on the integration issues that Scrum Teams experience. The *right people* are *the people who will do the work to resolve the cross-team issues the Nexus faces that day, or the ones supporting the people doing this work*; the Nexus Daily Scrum is not a "management" meeting at which topics get discussed and work gets delegated.

> *As the right representatives regroup, they realize that setting up the continuous integration environment really needs to be added to the Product Backlog; it is real work, it affects all the teams, and its status should be transparent. The Product Owner agrees, and they add it. They briefly discuss whether adding this puts the Nexus Goal at risk; fully automated continuous integration can take a lot of effort to implement.*
>
> *They agree they don't need a comprehensive continuous integration solution, they just need a common build and unit testing capability for now. They refine the continuous integration Product Backlog item into several smaller items to enable them to focus on the basics at first and a series of stepwise improvements that they can work on later. For now, having a common trunk-based branching strategy and common build and test environments will help the teams uncover issues early.*
>
> *The representatives of the teams agree that they will work together that day to consolidate the repositories and start using a common build server. There won't be a lot of code built today anyway, so now is a good time to make the change. With these agreements made, they go back to their own teams for their individual team Daily Scrum meetings.*[1]

---

1. For more on the Daily Scrum, see the article at https://dzone.com/articles/scrum-myths-daily-scrum-is-a-status-meeting.

This illustrates a couple of important points: The Nexus Daily Scrum makes the cross-team integration challenges transparent, so that the Scrum Teams can make the right decisions about how to handle the challenge. The Scrum Teams themselves will solve the problem, if it is within their power to solve. When this is not the case, the Scrum Master for the NIT supports the teams by reaching out to other parts of the organization, like operations or security, to get help. Failing that, the Scrum Master escalates issues to executive sponsors. Ultimately, however, the teams themselves are responsible for solving the problem.

The purpose of the Nexus Daily Scrum is to make integration issues transparent, but these issues need to be solved by the Scrum Teams working together, not by having the NIT solve problems for the Scrum Teams. Indeed, at this point in the case study, and as is often the case, the members of the NIT are also members of the Scrum Teams.

The second point of note is that the Nexus Daily Scrum is held *before* the Daily Scrum meetings of the Scrum Teams in the Nexus. This is the opposite of the order in the typical Scrum of Scrums approach in which Scrum Masters from separate Scrum Teams meet to coordinate work after the separate Scrum Team Daily Scrums.

The reason for this is that when the Nexus Daily Scrum exposes integration issues, the Scrum Teams usually will plan to work on different things than they would have before the integration issue surfaced. If they were to plan their daily work first and then have the Nexus Daily Scrum, their planning may be wasted because some more important integration issue needs to be addressed. The Nexus Daily Scrum helps the entire Nexus inspect and adapt by providing cross-team transparency.

The focus of the Nexus Daily Scrum on cross-team integration challenges sometimes creates a challenge knowing who should attend when the day's integration challenges aren't visible to all teams. Usually this is quickly solved with a brief discussion to make sure the right people will be able to attend.

The next day, a different issue comes up at the Nexus Daily Scrum: The Web/ Services Team needs to know from the other teams what kind of information they will be passing to the alerting service, and what kind of information they need from the service. They agree in the Nexus Daily Scrum to have a working session immediately to sketch out the kind of alerts they will need and what kind of information will be passed along. This will pull a few members from each team off their planned work for at least part of the day, so they adapt their plans in the team-level Daily Scrums.

This illustrates how the Nexus Daily Scrum helps the teams collaborate by providing a daily checkpoint to handle integration issues that have arisen, and why having team-level Daily Scrums naturally follows the Nexus Daily Scrum by helping the teams focus on integration issues first. Delaying the integration work can result in wasted effort or increased risk if the teams don't immediately address cross-team dependencies.

PROVIDING TRANSPARENCY INSIDE AND OUTSIDE THE NEXUS

The venture capitalist investors, among others, are interested in knowing whether their investments are going to pay off. They have three important questions they would like to have answered.

1. *How are things going?*
2. *What is the Nexus working on?*
3. *Have the priorities changed?*

To help answer these questions, the Nexus decides to introduce a simple mechanism to improve transparency. One of the Scrum Team members just came back from a workshop at which they were introduced to the concept of a Product Backlog "Treemap" (see Figure 5-2). The other members of the Nexus are intrigued by the representation and decided to try it out to learn more about it.

> With a little bit of work, they realize they could make it available to stakeholders on a secure product status website, with a link to the Product Backlog itself in case anyone wants to drill in for more detail. The Product Owner agrees to update the Product Backlog Treemap as soon as the teams have completed Product Backlog Items.
>
> They also decide, as a team, that the status of the build process is an important indicator of code health. This is too fine a level of detail for external stakeholders, but they want everyone on the team to see it so they create a separate web page just for the team. The NIT members agree to take on this work to help all of the Scrum Teams.

This illustrates something important about the NIT (whose members are usually also members of the Scrum Teams in the Nexus): They can pull together and do work when it helps the Nexus as a whole.

What this means in this situation is that the NIT members are going to reduce the amount of time they spend working in their Scrum Teams on PBIs to do some work that will benefit the Nexus. They get agreement from their Development Teams that this work will be a good thing, and so other team members either pick up some of the work or the teams agree to reduce their forecasts for the Sprint. Ultimately, regardless of who on the Nexus does this work, the Nexus must be able to answer these questions for its investors and stakeholders.

OPTIONAL PRACTICE: PRODUCT BACKLOG TREEMAP

Product Backlog Treemaps help to visualize the size/complexity and completeness of PBIs.[2] The sizes of the boxes represent the size of the PBI and coloring or shading is used to show completeness, with darker colors representing work that is more complete. It provides a quick overview of how "done" the work is, at a glance.

---

2. For more information about Product Backlog Treemaps, see https://www.mountaingoatsoftware.com/blog/visualizing-a-large-product-backlog-with-a-treemap.

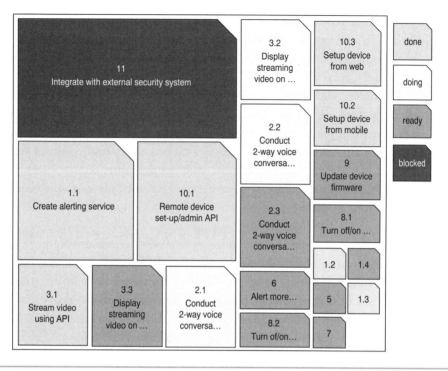

Figure 5-2 Product Backlog Treemap, as it might look in Sprint 3, showing the relative sizes and completeness of Product Backlog Items

This visualization can be easier to understand than a simple prioritized list-format Product Backlog (compare this to Figure 4-3). One complaint is that the Treemap is missing the priorities, but this lack is made up for by showing what is being worked on and how complete it is; stakeholders can defer to the Product Owner to make sure that the priorities are in order.

OPTIONAL PRACTICE: VISUALIZING PRODUCT BACKLOG BURNDOWN AND VELOCITY

A Product Backlog Burndown chart is frequently used to display progress as well, often with velocity, or the number of "points" (estimated earlier) delivered in each Sprint displayed alongside. While the chart is relatively intuitive, it can sometimes be confusing, such as when a large number of PBIs are added, causing the "burndown" to reverse, as is the case in Figure 5-3, where the first Sprint Review reveals functionality that was initially missed by the Product Owner but uncovered when the Product was shown to prospective customers in a Sprint Review.

A problem with Product Backlog Burndown charts that limits their usefulness is that truly depicting burndown requires that all PBIs be sized, which is rare because the task of estimating diverts attention from getting work done, and estimating is merely guessing anyway. The other problem is not with the chart but how it is sometimes misused, when people outside the Scrum Team use the information to judge performance instead of using it as a starting point for a discussion.

In addition, velocity and burndown, as well as Treemaps, require normalization of PBI sizing. Teams deciding to use techniques like these need to balance their value in providing transparency with the additional cost of estimate normalization. There is no ideal answer; teams will have to experiment and decide for themselves.

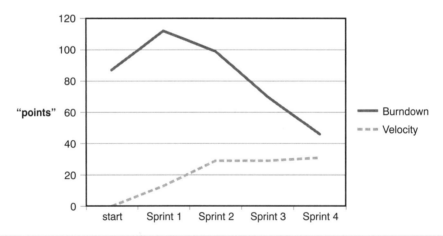

Figure 5-3 A Burndown-Velocity chart, showing the work remaining (burndown), and the work completed (velocity)

HOW MUCH PLANNING VISIBILITY IS ENOUGH?

The amount of reassurance stakeholders require generally depends on how much trust the Scrum Team has earned, how much money is at stake, and whether the initiative has been funded yet. A team that is unproven will generally have to provide a lot of support for their assertions about the cost of the Product and when they can release it. After they receive funding, they will still be closely watched by stakeholders to make sure that their estimates (on which the funding was based) are accurate. Until they release something, they will not have much credibility.

Conversely, a team that has earned the stakeholders' trust can get by with comparatively little planning: just enough to assure that they will deliver something of value with the money invested and the time available. Once the initiative is funded, they just need to provide reasonable assurances that they are on track for the release; often the current Nexus Sprint Backlog and rough sketches of the next couple of Sprints is sufficient (see Figure 5-4).

The lesson is simple: Teams that earn trust by delivering value don't have to spend as much time assuring stakeholders that things are going well—if they are transparent with their results and the results show steady progress.

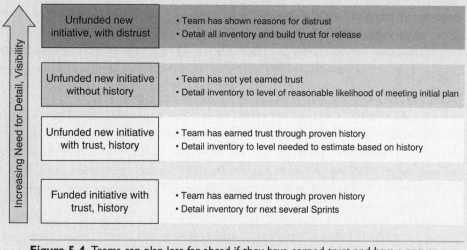

Figure 5-4 Teams can plan less far ahead if they have earned trust and have a proven track record

THE NEXUS SPRINT REVIEW

The Product Owner has been working with the Scrum Teams throughout the Sprint, looking at completed PBIs and verifying that the Integrated Product Increments the Nexus has been producing are truly done. Nevertheless, the Nexus Sprint Review is still useful to provide a snapshot of the state of the Product as a whole. It's also a chance to invite some of the investors to see that the Nexus has made good progress toward delivering a marketable product. All members of the Nexus attend, as this is their opportunity to hear what people think of their first integrated increment.

Since this is only the first Sprint, the state of the Product is rather rudimentary; the remote device configuration is currently done through APIs, but the API tests the team has developed show how the device can be administered through the APIs.

The alerting service is also rather rudimentary, but one of the developers has put together a demo showing how an alert raised, in this case by simulating having someone press the doorbell, triggers an alert that is then broadcast to his mobile device. It's not fancy, and there is no video or audio yet—just a text alert that the doorbell rang—but everyone is pleased at the progress, including the investors.

The investors present their views on what the market needs (supported by market research) and on potential competitors. This leads to a discussion about the doorbell/camera device: the prototype the Nexus has been working with is rather clunky, and everyone agrees that they will need something small, sleek, modern looking, and unobtrusive for the product to be a success in the market.

The investors offer that they have worked in the past with an offshore company in China that has a good track for delivering high-quality custom microelectronics at volume, at very low cost. The hardware team agrees that this could be a good option that they should investigate. They already had anticipated outsourcing the manufacturing, and getting a manufacturer involved earlier in the design process should avoid problems later.

The Nexus Sprint Review replaces the individual Scrum Team Sprint Reviews, and everyone in the Nexus attends, as well as any external stakeholders who are interested; even prospective customers or users may be invited. This can make organizing them challenging, especially when not everyone may be at the same location. In addition, with multiple teams contributing during the Sprint, not everything that was done can realistically be reviewed.

The entire Nexus participates in the Nexus Sprint Review. This is their chance to show what they've achieved and to get feedback from stakeholders and other interested parties, to broadly share information, and to learn. It's not just about demonstration.

OPTIONAL PRACTICE: USING THE "EXPOSITION" (EXPO) FORMAT FOR NEXUS SPRINT REVIEWS

In the "Expo" (or "Science Fair") format, all the Scrum Teams and review participants gather in a single large room. The Scrum Teams set up a number of separate stations at which they demonstrate different aspects of what they have accomplished during the Sprint. In our case study, if they had more to show, they could have one station demonstrating the mobile app, another showing the web app, and another showing the physical device. Organizing stations by persona makes it easier to understand how different kinds of people will use the product, which leads to more focused feedback.

OPTIONAL PRACTICE: USING OFFLINE REVIEW TECHNIQUES FOR NEXUS SPRINT REVIEWS

Offline Sprint Reviews, including Nexus Sprint Reviews, are useful in cases where stakeholders aren't able to attend the Sprint Review either because of scheduling conflicts or because they are located remote from where the Sprint Review is being held.

Several techniques can be useful to engage remote participants.

- **Record the demonstrations for playback.** Demos can be recorded using a variety of technologies to show screen interactions, narrated by a commentator to provide context. Preparing the demo videos is also a good motivator for testing as it forces the developers to create and test the end-to-end story. A big disadvantage with recorded demonstration is the missing direct feedback from the stakeholders for the Nexus.
- **Circulate videos before the Sprint Review.** Sharing these ahead of time can yield useful feedback before the Sprint Review that may help improve it, and it may motivate a stakeholder to make time to attend the in-person Sprint Review.

- **Keep the videos short.** A minute or two for a specific feature is sufficient to respect stakeholder time commitments.

- **Provide a way for remote participants to give feedback, and follow up with them on actions taken.** Knowing that their feedback made a difference motivates stakeholders to participate in the future, either remotely or in person.

There is no one single "best" Nexus Sprint Review practice; other popular techniques include Open Spaces and World Cafés. Mixing it up with different techniques helps to keep reviews fresh. Using the same approach, Sprint after Sprint, becomes tiring, and stakeholders can lose interest. The important thing is to engage people to give feedback and to keep the review from feeling like a "phase-gate approval" process.

The feedback from the Nexus Sprint Review results in the Product Owner making adjustments to the Product Backlog. She adds a PBI to develop and deliver a doorbell device that meets customer aesthetic requirements, company profitability goals, and security and reliability goals.

NEXUS SPRINT RETROSPECTIVE

Retrospectives serve two purposes: to recognize successful practices that the Scrum Teams are already using, and to help them find ways they can improve. The first part is important but often forgotten, and good Scrum Masters will help their teams by calling out reasons to celebrate when they forget to do so themselves. The second part, looking for ways to improve, is both easier and harder: easier because finding faults is natural for many people, and harder because finding ways to improve requires thoughtful analysis and deliberate action.

The Nexus Sprint Retrospective process has three parts, as shown in Figure 5-5.

Figure 5-5 The Nexus Sprint Retrospective process

1. Appropriate members from the Scrum Teams meet to identify issues that have affected more than one team.

2. Each Scrum Team meets to hold their own Retrospective on how they did as a team. Their discussion includes the cross-team issues that have been raised in the Nexus Sprint Retrospective.

3. Appropriate members from the Scrum Teams then get together. After each team has done its own Sprint Retrospective, the NIT looks at the consolidated results to look for common themes and to decide what actions need to be taken.

Because there are common scaling dysfunctions, every Retrospective should address the following questions.

- Have they met the Nexus Goal? If not, why not?
- Was any work left undone? Did the Nexus generate technical debt?
- Were all artifacts, particularly code, frequently (ideally, continuously) and successfully integrated?
- Was the software successfully built, tested, and deployed often enough to prevent the overwhelming accumulation of unresolved dependencies?

When issues are discovered, the representatives need to ask:

- Why did this happen?
- How can the issue be fixed?
- How can recurrence be prevented?

Following the Nexus Sprint Review, Scrum Team members who have particular insights into the integration challenges the teams have faced meet to conduct a Nexus Retrospective, focusing on cross-team integration issues, facilitated by the Nexus Scrum Master. There the participants share the issues they faced that they think the Scrum Teams need to consider more deeply. Several themes emerge: Having one team responsible for all common services seems to be becoming a bottleneck for the other teams, and having teams responsible for components seems to be causing similar problems.

After the initial Nexus Sprint Retrospective session has finished, each Scrum Team in the Nexus conducts its own Scrum Sprint Retrospective. They focus on issues that have uniquely affected them, as well as the cross-team and integration issues that came up in the first part of the Nexus Sprint Retrospective. This supports bottom-up intelligence, allowing the teams closest to the work to suggest improvements that may affect everyone. Often, Scrum Teams will use a Retrospective Board similar to Figure 5-6 on which any team member can post notes to any of the areas.

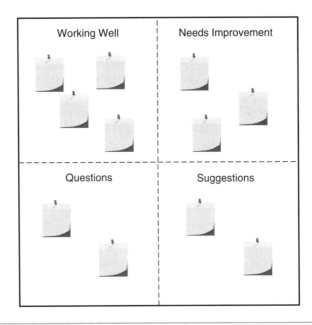

Figure 5-6 A simple Sprint Retrospective Board

The result of the discussion is a set of actions that they can take to improve, and a plan to implement the actions that only affect their team. To the extent that improvement only affects a single team, this part of the overall Nexus Sprint Retrospective is just like Scrum.

> After each team has done its own Sprint Retrospective, the NIT gets back together for the final part of the Nexus Sprint Retrospective. They want to consolidate their findings on cross-team issues, looking for common themes.
>
> In the "Working Well" category, they found the Nexus Daily Scrum useful in finding cross-team issues. They also found that the cross-team dependency analysis had helped them plan the Sprint more effectively. They felt that pairing with members from the Mobile Team was useful in giving people broader understanding of that part of the Product, and that they would be able to spread work across the Nexus more effectively. They also found that the continuous integration process was working well, although more of the testing needs to be automated.
>
> In the "Needs Improvement" category, they have realized that having one team responsible for all services is a bottleneck; they had already seen how the demand for services is growing faster than any one team can respond. They felt it was time to move to a "feature team" model.[3]
>
> They all agree that they will need a better way of deploying across web, mobile, and device platforms in a coordinated way, both for new releases as well as patches, both for testing as well as to real customers once the product is shipping. Finally, they decide they need a better way to share knowledge and experiences across teams.
>
> In the "Suggestions" category, they knew they needed to get better at automated testing. And in the "Questions" category, they need to get some help on how to further investigate outsourcing the hardware from the venture capital firm.
>
> They pull the information together on a Retrospective Board that they can leave on a whiteboard in one of the team rooms (see Figure 5-7).

---

3. In a "feature team" model, any team can work on any PBI, which may or may not actually be a feature. For a lengthy and passionate discussion about feature teams, see https://www.scrum.org/forum/scrum-forum/5563/feature-teams-vs-component-teams.

When they start their final Nexus Retrospective session, everything starts out in the "Plan" column; the improvement ideas have to be discussed. As they work through them, they decide that they definitely want to move to Feature Teams, so they move that card to the "Do" column. The same goes for improving the Continuous Delivery process and tools and for exploring outsourcing the device design and manufacturing.

They think that is about all they can do. Moving to Feature Teams feels like a big deal, but they decide to experiment with the Web/Service and Mobile Teams. They had already been heading in this direction, but they decide to try to push the experiment further in the next Sprint. They will leave the board up, and anyone, at any time, can add cards to the "Plan" column.

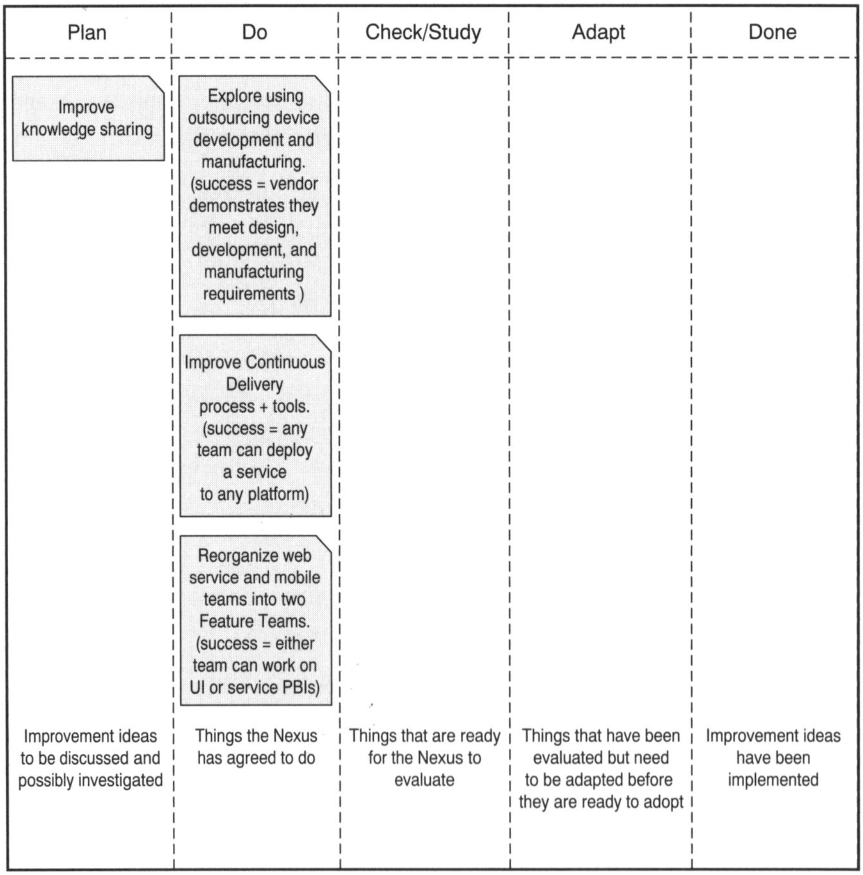

Plan	Do	Check/Study	Adapt	Done
Improve knowledge sharing	Explore using outsourcing device development and manufacturing. (success = vendor demonstrates they meet design, development, and manufacturing requirements)			
	Improve Continuous Delivery process + tools. (success = any team can deploy a service to any platform)			
	Reorganize web service and mobile teams into two Feature Teams. (success = either team can work on UI or service PBIs)			
Improvement ideas to be discussed and possibly investigated	Things the Nexus has agreed to do	Things that are ready for the Nexus to evaluate	Things that have been evaluated but need to be adapted before they are ready to adopt	Improvement ideas have been implemented

Figure 5-7 A Plan-Do-Check-Adapt Sprint Retrospective Board

As the items are completed, they will be moved into the Check/Study column, at which time the Nexus will decide whether the improvement is ready to be adopted or needs adjustment. Once it is done, it is moved to the "Done" column or simply removed from the board.[4] As the Nexus plans its next Sprint, it will need to allow for the time it will spend making these improvements when it estimates its capacity.

With the Nexus Retrospective concluded, they have a plan for how they will improve in the next Sprint, which continues in Chapter 6, "Evolving the Nexus."

CLOSING

Transparency is easier to achieve in Scrum because the natural effects of collaboration between team members exposes many issues, and the Daily Scrum helps to expose those issues that don't surface naturally. When many teams need to collaborate, exposing cross-team issues is harder because issues can remain hidden for a long time unless deliberately brought to light. The timing of the Nexus Daily Scrum, before the team-level Daily Scrums, helps to flush the cross-team issues into the open.

Providing transparency to stakeholders is also more challenging. Even the Product Owner can struggle with understanding where all the teams in the Nexus are at any given time. Providing ways for anyone to understand progress and issues, at any point in time, improves transparency and reduces interruptions.

Nexus Sprint Reviews can also become more challenging as the numbers of teams and stakeholders grow. To achieve the review in the timebox, the Nexus often has to be selective and creative about what it shows to make sure that everyone is able to see what interests them. Formal review events are not the only time the teams should elicit feedback, and continuous engagement provides not only full transparency but also the benefit of earlier feedback.

---

4. For more information, see http://www.ontheagilepath.net/2015/08/what-about-your-retrospective-action-items-use-the-active-learning-cycle-or-plan-do-check-act-board.html.

With many teams engaged, the Nexus Sprint Retrospective requires more structure than the simpler single-team Scrum Retrospective. Canvassing cross-team issues before the team Retrospectives provides them with some starting points for their discussions. Coming back together after the team Retrospectives makes sure that cross-team issues receive attention once they are raised.

EVOLVING 6 THE NEXUS

Healthy teams evolve over time. Team members change, stakeholders change, and even the work itself changes as the teams learn more about themselves, the technology, and what customers really need. Scrum and Nexus help teams to *inspect and adapt* not just the product that they are building, but also the way that they work together.

Varying the team structure and composition is healthy, to a point. Teams do take time to form, build trust, and develop the relationships that help them perform at high levels. They also can stagnate over time, become insular, and become less capable of dealing with change. Healthy teams achieve a balance between stability and change to improve their ability to meet new challenges.

The Nexus works through a few more Sprints, learning more about how to work together. During these Sprints, they grapple with a fundamental question: How can they balance the workload better across all teams? Their experience with teams organized around components has been uneven. It has been hard to balance the workload across teams, yet they feel constrained by their perceived need for

> *component-specific expertise. At their last Retrospective, they discussed the topic of organizing teams around Features rather than components, and they agreed the idea was worth trying. They have been rotating people through teams enough that they think that each team may have broad enough skills to make it work.*

WHY COMPONENT TEAMS CAN BECOME A PROBLEM

Many organizations come to Scrum with a team structure that is component oriented.[1] Sometimes this is because developing a component requires knowledge that not all teams have, as in the example, or where developing a component requires special security clearances, as can be the case when developing components with high commercial or political/military sensitivity.

More often, component ownership is merely an historical accident, the result of that team having originally developed the component. In organizations where teams work on many projects at once, a team may own many different components. When one of the components needs to be modified, they dust off their old component knowledge and make the necessary changes. Their availability to work on the component may even delay an entire project. Scheduling work and managing component-project-team dependencies keeps many Program Management Offices very busy indeed.

A strong indicator that organizing around components is no longer working is that the teams find it increasingly hard to balance the workload among themselves. Symptoms of this increasing complexity include the following.

1. **A highly serialized development life cycle, with poor time to market.** Component team work has to be planned with very high precision, in a very specific order, for a product to be delivered. When unexpected changes are needed, schedule changes and slippage ensue.

2. **A high number of cross-team handoffs and a large amount of Work In Process.** This serialization means that many changes must be done before anything can be delivered, and when a change occurs much of the work already done may have to be re-done or scrapped.

---

1. "Conway's Law" is the observation that any organization that designs a system (defined broadly) will produce a design whose structure is a copy of the organization's communication structure. For more information, see http://www.melconway.com/Home/Conways_Law.html.

3. **Complex and often ineffective dependency management.** Coordinating component teams requires lots of project or program management overhead that adds cost.

4. **Working on low-value features.** When teams have no better work to do, they tend to create work for themselves "improving" the components they own.

5. **Opaque measure of progress.** When the work is fragmented across many teams, the organization finds it hard to see where the real value is. Everyone can be very busy but customers are still unhappy.

6. **Poor quality.** "High quality" means not just absence of defects, but also ability to meet the needs of customers. When work is fragmented across teams, it's hard to see that these teams are not working on things that make a difference to customers.

DEVELOPMENT TEAMS IN SCRUM CONSIST OF MORE THAN "DEVELOPERS"

One of Scrum's roles is the *Development Team*. Some interpret this name to mean that it consists only of people who write code. Great Development Teams need lots of skills beyond just coding, although they need to be able to deliver code as well. User eXperience (UX) skills help the team better understand customers and deliver great solutions. Operations skills help the team understand how the product will be deployed and supported. Testing skills help the team validate the code they've developed. The key to making this all work is having cross-functional team members, not narrow specialists. In an ideal team, everyone should be able to contribute in many different dimensions.

OPTIONAL PRACTICE: ORGANIZING SCRUM TEAMS AROUND FEATURES

To form new teams around features, all the members of the Nexus get together. The Scrum Master of the NIT sets the stage by asking team members to form three groups with all the skills they would need to develop any feature or to update any component.[2]

---

2. To learn more about self-organizing teams, see "Creating Great Teams; How Self-Selection Lets People Excel" by Sandy Mamoli and David Mole.

> *People naturally group together with people with whom they want to work at first, and the groups start out a little unbalanced; they resemble the original component teams. The Scrum Master asks the groups questions about whether they could work on anything, whether they have all the skills they need. Finally, where a team has more than enough skills, someone with skills that another team needs switches teams. The self-sorting process works itself out in about a half an hour.*

Self-organization is important because it empowers teams to make decisions and be accountable. Holding teams accountable for their own results means giving them the freedom to make decisions, and team membership is the foundation for all future collaboration.

> *The teams are not completely balanced yet. Pairing mobile team members with device team members in the first Sprint helped to spread some of the knowledge, but not everyone has worked on the services layer yet. To help solve this problem, developers with service layer experience spread themselves across the teams. They will work within their new teams to spread knowledge on developing the services over the next couple of Sprints.*

Feature teams are cross-functional teams that are responsible for the end-to-end delivery of product features or capabilities, as guided by the Product Owner. They are free to change or add code across the entire software stack. Adopting a Feature Team approach requires the Product source code be managed in an open way, so that any authorized team member can modify the code (see Figure 6-1).

OPTIONAL PRACTICE: MANAGING CODE LIKE AN OPEN-SOURCE PROJECT

Using an "open source"-like coding approach requires organizational commitment and greater developer discipline. Organizations that adopt it typically have very strong mentoring cultures, and they make time for developers to share with other developers. They often adopt pair programming techniques to help developers learn good techniques from one another.

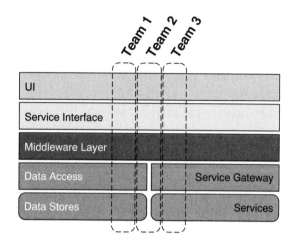

Figure 6-1 Feature Teams are responsible for the end-to-end delivery of product features or capabilities

They also put safeguards around the code, including having designated committers who decide what code gets accepted, and peer code reviews to enforce but also to socialize code quality standards. These organizations also tend to have robust and mature continuous integration practices, including automated unit and regression testing. With the right practices, open code management approaches deliver better solutions with much higher quality and a better ability to balance work across teams.

Feature teams display the following characteristics.

- They are largely independent, self-sufficient, and self-organized. Based on their combined skills and past experience they may be uniquely qualified for specific work, so they may have some similarities to teams formed around specialty knowledge. In the example, because certain features are mostly aligned with areas of technical specialty, the same team structure would mostly satisfy both approaches.

- They can incubate a component and even serve as its steward, but they don't own it exclusively.

- They may be responsible for multiple functional/feature areas, especially if the product is relatively small.

If a PBI is too large for one team, other teams in the Nexus pitch in to help.[3] When this happens, each team develops some unique aspect of the feature while minimizing dependencies; the team who started work on the feature or develops its main part retains overall responsibility.

Organizing teams around features provides a number of benefits.

- **More flexible design decisions.** Component teams often get stuck pursuing one solution; the more people who work on the code, the better the chance that someone may see a better solution.
- **Reduced waste caused by handoffs.** The more handoffs, the more delays and waste in the delivery process.
- **Reduced unplanned work.** When team members do have to wait, they find things to keep them busy...and not always work that leads to delivering value. Unplanned work is a silent killer of productivity.
- **Better time to market.** Fewer handoffs, less wait time, and better ability to balance work across teams help organizations shorten the feedback cycle of building, delivering, getting feedback, and adapting their products based on that feedback.
- **Reduced integration overhead.** Most component teams delay integration instead of continuously integrating the full product. This often happens when they work in large batches, collecting a lot of changes to do all at once rather than making changes continuously. When teams delay integration, they create complexity and rework when the code does not integrate.
- **Increased customer focus.** Feature teams deliver things that matter to customers, forcing teams to understand what customers need, and to find ways to better serve the customers. Component teams just work on cogs in the machine; they rarely interact with real users or customers, they are just handed specifications on what to build. Component teams result in a situation in which everyone is busy but no one is focused on the user or customer.

---

3. While Scrum Teams are ideally composed of 7±2 members, there is nothing wrong with having fewer than 3 members or more than 9. As teams grow larger, they tend to fragment, lose cohesion, and become less effective. Twenty is most certainly too many, but a team with 10 or 11 members may work perfectly fine.

- **Increased code quality.** With feature teams, all teams work on all parts of the code base, and as such they are all accountable for keeping quality of the entire code base high. In addition, developers write better code because they work on the problem holistically instead of developing components in isolation. Better code and better designs means easier to maintain code.

- **Stronger developers.** Developers learn more about a broad range of technical issues and don't get stuck in narrow technical specialties.

OPTIONAL PRACTICE: ORGANIZING TEAMS AROUND PERSONAS

One strategy for organizing teams is to have a team develop PBIs related to a particular theme or customer journey. An easy way to establish a theme is using personas. A persona is a summary description of a particular kind of user. They are often given names and specific biographical details to help make them more tangible.[4] Aligning teams with personas can be useful when a Product delivers value to several different and very distinct personas, and when the PBIs are closely aligned with a particular persona. Over time, aligning teams with personas helps the team developer greater understanding of, and empathy for, the persona, which helps them develop better solutions for their persona(s) (see Figure 6-2).

> *Several of the Nexus members had worked on feature teams before and had positive experiences. One team member observed: "Most of my development experience has been on teams where I worked on components that other teams used. While the things I built made it into products, I never got any direct feedback from real users or customers. When I've had the chance to work on things that people use more directly, I felt a lot better about my work, and I was much more motivated to better understand what they really needed."*

---

4. For more information on personas and how they can be used to better understand customers, see http://www.jeffgothelf.com/blog/using-personas-for-executive-alignment/.

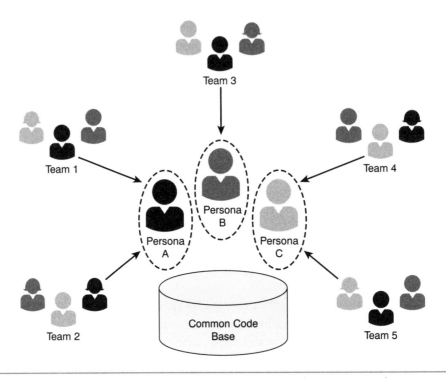

Figure 6-2 Forming teams around personas can improve a team's connection with customers

Despite these benefits, organizations can find it challenging, at least in the near term, to have any team be able to work on any PBIs. Sometimes, a team will lack the domain expertise to work on some areas of the code, especially involving aspects that require advanced mathematics, scientific or engineering knowledge, or knowledge of a particular application. In the long run, these challenges can be overcome by cross-training team members and encouraging team members to learn new skills.

Other situations, for instance, those involving high levels of security clearance or desire for secrecy, may require separation of duties that precludes organizing into feature teams. Pair programming and rotating developers between teams can help to spread knowledge between teams in ways that can reduce team specialization over time, but some barriers may be impossible to overcome. When rotating team members between teams, it is important to balance the benefits of rotating with the benefits of stable teams.

EXPANDING THE NEXUS INTEGRATION TEAM

> *During the Nexus Sprint Retrospective, the teams identified that they wanted to improve their continuous delivery capability, ultimately to be able to deploy any component to any platform (web/cloud, iOS, Android, and the device). To help with this, one of the team members recommends a consultant who could help the Nexus with this, someone they worked with at a previous company. One of the NIT members helps by making contact and coordinating the contract. The teams and the continuous integration/continuous delivery (CI/CD) consultant decide that he should become part of the NIT to best support all the teams in the Nexus.*

NIT members don't always come from the Nexus itself; sometimes they come from other parts of the organization, or even outside the organization, as is the case here. The NIT provides the Nexus with a mechanism for sharing people and resources across the entire Nexus. Since the CI/CD infrastructure will benefit all the teams, having the consultant who is helping set it up be part of the NIT is a good way to make sure the work benefits all teams.

These "external" members of the NIT may be shared with other parts of the organization so long as they are able to work for the Nexus whenever needed. Their "outside" work would not be represented on the Product Backlog because it does not benefit the Product. The main challenge the NIT faces when it brings in outside members is negotiating and ensuring their commitment to be available to the Nexus when the Nexus needs them. This means that supporting the Nexus has to be their top priority; they need to put everything else on hold to support the Nexus. If they can't do this, they can't be part of the NIT.

UPDATING AND REFINING THE PRODUCT BACKLOG

> *Following the first Sprint, the Product Owner updates and reorders the Product Backlog. Evaluating and selecting a partner to design and manufacture the hardware has become the top priority, and the web client interfaces have become less important and may be dropped entirely for the first release. The thinking*

behind this is that the main value of the product is for people to know when someone has come to the house while they are away or when someone is walking around the house. The web interfaces can wait until later (see Figure 6-3).

Product Backlog refinement now happens continuously, triggered when new PBIs are identified or when a team learns something new that may change its estimate of how complex a PBI is.

Product Backlog Items

12 – Evaluate and select a design/manufacturing partner
1 – Alert user(s) that doorbell has been rung
  1.2 – Respond to button press (ring bell, raise #doorbellRung alert)
  1.3 – Detect #doorbellRung alert event, notify mobile user
2 – Conduct conversation with visitor through doorbell speaker using mobile device
  2.1 – Conduct conversation with visitor through doorbell speaker using mobile device (iOS)
  2.2 – Conduct conversation with visitor through doorbell speaker using mobile device (Android)
14 – Automate the deployment of a new product version
  14.3 – Automate the deployment of a cloud service
3 – View selected security camera over web or mobile device
  3.1 – Stream video using standard open source API
  3.2 – Display streaming video on mobile device using standard open source API
13 – Choose cloud platform vendor
14 – Deploy new product version
  14.1 – Deploy iOS application
  14.2 – Deploy Android application
  14.4 – Update customer device firmware
8 – Turn off/on alerts for a mobile or web client
  8.2 – Turn off/on alerts for web client
10 – Setup/admin device from web or mobile phone
  10.2 – set-up/admin device from mobile phone
5 – Generate #motion Detected alert
11 – Integrate with external security systems
  11.1 – Identify, evaluate, and partner with external security service provider
  11.2 – Integrate site management features with external security service provider systems
3 – View selected security camera over web or mobile device
  3.3 – Display streaming video in web browser using standard open source API
2 – Conduct conversation with visitor through doorbell speaker
  2.3 – Conduct 2-way voice conversation via universal client API in web browser session
10 – Setup/admin device from web or mobile phone
  10.3 – Setup/admin device from web
1 – Alert user(s) that doorbell has been rung
  1.4 – Detect #doorbellRung alert event, notify web user

Figure 6-3 Updated Product Backlog with PBI goals for the current Sprint in black text

There is a PBI dependency that is worrisome—PBI #2 depends on PBI #1. The teams figure out that this is not as worrisome as it looks—one team can work on alerting while the other team can work on the two-way communication, and late in the Sprint they can enable the alert to start a two-way communication; initially, it can simply be an acknowledgement. They will use the Nexus Daily Scrum to coordinate between teams and keep the work in sync.

The Nexus has a lively discussion about whether automating deployment should be put on the Product Backlog, or whether it is just a task in the Sprint Backlog that simply needs to be done. The Product Owner initially questions whether this is really critical to the product. Several team members argue that being able to quickly deploy security fixes or product enhancements is something that will improve customer satisfaction. The Product Owner agrees that this is an important product capability, so she adds it to the Product Backlog.

While the Product Owner is accountable for updating and reordering the Product Backlog, he or she can enlist the help of other people on the team to do the work. In addition, the Product Owner is not the sole source of insight on things that might make the Product better; high-performing teams often engage in healthy discussion about just that topic. And although the Product Owner has the final say on inclusion and priorities, other team members often propose ideas that help to shape and evolve the Product Backlog.

NEXUS SPRINT PLANNING, REVISITED

With the newly formed teams, Nexus Sprint Planning for the second Sprint proceeds much like the previous Nexus Sprint Planning session. The Product Owner establishes the Nexus Goal for the Sprint as having the basic alerting and two-way conversation functionality working, as well as having a manufacturing partner selected. The teams feel comfortable with their forecast, although the Scrum Master on the NIT cautions about the potential productivity drop associated with forming new teams. The teams understand his concerns but feel that newly formed Scrum teams won't affect productivity much.[5]

There will also be a couple of team members helping to evaluate potential manufacturing partners. They need a partner who will be able to fully participate in the Nexus as well as one who can produce a device with the software interfaces they have defined (the same events and alerts). There are a couple of manufacturers who claim they can do this, but the team needs to prove that the software interfaces won't change (or if they will change, to understand how much rework will be created). The Product Owner will also participate in the partner selection process.

The addition of outside members on the NIT does not change Nexus Sprint Planning; rather, it amplifies the importance of planning. Having the outside NIT members participate in Nexus Sprint Planning helps raise issues that the teams might have otherwise missed. In the case here, the existing Nexus team members don't have much experience evaluating manufacturing partners, so the addition of outside expertise helps them to understand how much time they will need to spend on evaluation tasks.

THE NEXUS DAILY SCRUM, TAKE TWO

Once the Nexus has organized into feature teams, new coordination challenges arise. With anyone able to modify code in the code base, they risk unintentionally creating merge conflicts that will take extra work to resolve. They decide they can best avoid this by using the Nexus Daily Scrum to alert other teams that a developer will be working on a particular component that day. When these situations occur, the developers can talk to one another and decide that they can work around each other's access or, when this isn't possible, they can temporarily pair up to work on the same component.

---

5. Perhaps the best-known model of group development was developed by Bruce Tuckman in 1965. For more information, see https://en.wikipedia.org/wiki/Tuckman's_stages_of_group_development.

The Nexus Daily Scrum also helps the teams share knowledge in cases where one team needs to work on an unfamiliar part of the code, by having people who have knowledge of a particular part of the code base collaborate with people who are still learning about it. An example of this occurs one day when one team asks for help with modifying a service that someone on another team had developed in an earlier Sprint. They agree that the developers will pair today until the one who needs to better understand the code feels comfortable making the change.

Finally, the Nexus Daily Scrum also becomes a useful daily touch point for improving continuous-delivery practices and automation: representatives from the development teams raise issues they are having with the continuous-delivery pipeline and agree how they will work together and with the continuous-delivery consultant (an external member of the NIT) during the day to resolve them. The consultant works with the team working on the PBI to automate the deployment of a cloud service, and members of other teams working on cloud services help as part of their effort to ensure that every service they build has automated tests to detect problems early in the delivery pipeline.

The Nexus Daily Scrum does not take the place of collaboration; its raises the visibility of the need to collaborate and to provide the Scrum Teams with a way to focus the collaboration by making issues and potential conflicts more transparent.

It also becomes a focal point for interacting with external members of the NIT by giving the external experts a single point of contact with all the Scrum Teams. As the number of teams in a Nexus grows, having simpler ways for these external team members to engage with teams becomes more important. The Nexus Daily Scrum isn't the place where all inter-team and external team member interactions take place, but it does provide a time and a place where the Nexus identifies the need for more collaboration.

THE NEXUS SPRINT REVIEW, TAKE TWO

The Nexus Sprint Review reveals good progress but also shines a light on some growing problems.

A hardware partner has been identified, and the team was able to create a working prototype of a new webcam-enabled doorbell using the hardware partner's device platform. The new platform will enable smaller, more aesthetically pleasing hardware that will give designers more flexibility. The collaboration with the vendor was good, and the vendor indicated that they would be able to add their own team to the Nexus in the future.

The Nexus also demonstrated the ability to broadcast an alert to a mobile phone when the doorbell was rung, and then conducting a two-way voice conversation between the mobile device and the doorbell device...on iOS. The same feature on Android was not yet working, as the teams encountered some unexpected difficulties. The Product Owner and VC stakeholders felt what was demonstrated on iOS was valuable and worked well, which was important because this feature was one of the key selling points of the product. Making it work on Android is important to make sure the product will be viable in the market.

The Nexus also demonstrated using the continuous-delivery pipeline automation to deploy a new or changed service to the cloud; anytime a change was made in the source repository, the service was built and deployed. While the concept worked, the Product Owner wanted to have a way to manually review the test results before deployment to make sure that the service was adequately tested before it was released.

Failing to achieve the Nexus Goal for a Sprint—in this case, demonstrating differentiating capabilities like being able to receive alerts and conduct two-way voice conversations on both iOS and Android—is always cause for concern: Is it part of some broader trend, or just an isolated incident? Is there an underlying problem that needs to be addressed? The causes will be examined in the Nexus Sprint Retrospective; for the purposes of the Nexus Review, the main problem is managing expectations and not being either too optimistic about progress or undisciplined about not taking on more work than is reasonably possible to achieve.

THE NEXUS SPRINT RETROSPECTIVE, TAKE TWO

> *Some problems lurked beneath the surface of what appeared to be a mostly successful Nexus Sprint Review. Even though the Nexus had mostly hit their Nexus Goal, with the exception of the voice conversation feature on Android, there was an uneasiness that the next Sprint would not go better.*
>
> *Team formation was more difficult than expected. The trust and transparency that had been present in the component teams had frayed a bit with the current teams. The main issue was code quality. Some of the code was pretty ugly. It worked, but it really needed to be reworked, and the intense pressure to implement new features prevented the teams from making progress on this. Frustration was growing, along with growing technical debt. Where the Component Teams had been "performing," to use Tuckman's teaming model, they were now knocked back to "storming," and it confused them.*
>
> *All of this came to a head in the Nexus Sprint Retrospective. The Scrum Master on the NIT had his hands full keeping the discussion from degenerating into frustrated finger pointing.*

Tuckman's model of team formation provides useful insights into the challenges teams face in building the trust and transparency that is essential to high performance (see Figure 6-4).

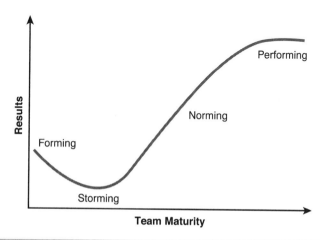

Figure 6-4 Team formation goes through predictable stages

At the *forming* stage, team members are still getting to know one another. They haven't yet built the trust and transparency they need to deliver their best results. They may cling to old roles or old behavior patterns, such as the developer who feels uncomfortable raising issues in the Daily Scrum because he doesn't yet feel comfortable asking for help, or the Business Analyst turned Product Owner who wants assurances that all her requirements will be delivered by the final release date. In a small organization, they may still largely identify with their former team membership.

When teams are under pressure to produce, this quickly gives way to *storming*. They experience a lot of conflict; they are experiencing the pain of not working very effectively, and this frustrates them; they *should* be able to be more effective. They require a lot of coaching and encouragement, and sometimes even conflict resolution. Without help and support, they can easily get stuck here.

In the *norming* stage, the team members determine how they will cooperate. They form working relationships, they establish boundaries and norms, and they build the trust and transparency they need to deliver results.

In the *performing* stage, they have built the trust and relationships that enable them to deliver their best results.

TOO MUCH WORK, NOT ENOUGH PROGRESS

> *Another problem that was obvious is that while the mobile developers had a lot of iOS experience, hence the great progress on that part of the demonstration, they lacked Android experience. When they started to look at what implementing on Android meant, they realized that it was not going to be a simple "port."*

Not making progress as expected is not unique to teams in a Nexus; any Scrum Team can experience the same problem. Everyone struggles with taking on too much work or not being realistic about how much they can achieve. It is easy for people to underestimate the effort required to deliver PBIs and easy to make assumptions, like the one about Android development being just like iOS development.

In this case, the NIT and the Scrum Master bear responsibility for helping the teams to be more realistic. There is a fine line, however, between helping someone understand and telling them what to do; the former is empowering, and the latter undermines team self-organization by going back to a more traditional management style. Sometimes the right thing to do is to let a team take on too much work so its members learn their realistic limits.

GROWING TECHNICAL DEBT

> To solve the Android development problem, they realized they needed to develop a common device-independent layer, or they needed to find a framework that provides device independence, which still meant refactoring their existing code. With the pressure to deliver, however, they didn't have time to do either. Now they can see the impact of not having such a platform, and they realize that they need to rework a lot of the code they have written.

Dealing with technical debt is like exercise: Everyone knows they should do it, but people are often too busy to make it a part of their daily lives.[6] Scrum Teams, including members of a Nexus, are no different. They find it easier and more rewarding to work on new PBIs, and they gain satisfaction from completing them. Dealing with technical debt feels like having to clean one's house: It's messy and unpleasant, and often more complex than new development work. Nevertheless, it is important.

Transparency is the first step to solving this problem: making everyone aware that it exists, and helping the Product Owner understand why making time to reduce technical debt is as important as working on other PBIs.

UNAVAILABLE PRODUCT OWNER

> They also experienced some problems when the Product Owner was not as available as needed, due to her work helping with the hardware partner search.

---

6. For a deeper discussion of technical debt, see Martin Fowler's blog on the topic: https://martinfowler.com/bliki/TechnicalDebt.html.

When they have challenges scaling, some organizations are tempted to assign multiple Product Owners to a single Product, perhaps with a hierarchy of Product Owners (e.g., having a "Lead" Product Owner, with "subordinate" Product Owners).

This can be confusing when it is unclear who makes decisions or who is accountable, or when it degenerates into a Product Owner committee.

The Product Owner is the single person accountable for the ultimate direction and success of the Product. Let that sink in. That means that the Product Owner must:

- Establish a clear and compelling vision for the Product
- Empower the Development Team to deliver that vision so it they can look less to the Product Owner for constant decision making
- Enlist the help of the Scrum Master to help the Development Team
- Make decisions about the vision or the progress of the Product toward that vision
- Work with stakeholders
- Research the market, understand customers, and everything else needed to ensure that the Development Team is building the right product

The Product Owner *can*, however, involve other people in helping to clarify details and to provide subject matter expertise. She can have other people help to refine the backlog and represent her when she can't be present. She can delegate tasks but not accountability. She retains final say even when she can't be everywhere at once; the Product Owner can enlist helpers or surrogates, so long as she retains the final decision authority.

INADEQUATE BUILD AND TEST AUTOMATION

An outcome from the individual team retrospectives was that while the continuous integration process is working, developers haven't been spending enough time automating tests for a continuous delivery process to really work. The process worked well enough for the simple services delivered during the Sprint, but

> *without more robust automated tests the process will simply deploy poorly tested code more quickly. As with the other issues, the pressure to deliver new capabilities is outstripping their ability to deliver with high quality.*

Traditionally, in the rush to develop new features, developers frequently shortchange testing, relegating it to the "if we have time" task category. To avoid this, testing should be part of the definition of "Done" for each PBI, including:

- Unit tests
- Acceptance tests
- Performance and scalability tests
- Security tests
- Deployment tests...and so forth

Automating these tests can be expensive, but because Scrum Teams build and test software all the time, investing in automation quickly pays off in reduced manual testing cost and improved reliability. Early detection of problems also dramatically reduces cost by reducing time spent finding and fixing problems later, when the developer has to recreate the context of the breaking changes. Automating testing and making it part of the continuous integration process is essential to keeping code clean when many teams are working in the same code base. In fact, continuous integration without automated tests is just compilation.

FORMING A PLAN TO IMPROVE

> *For the next Sprint, to deal with the rework problem, the teams decide that they need to set aside 20% of their capacity to deal with rework, refactoring, and other work related to reducing technical debt. They also get the Product Owner to agree that when they identify critical rework that can't be accomplished within the same Sprint, they will put it on the Product Backlog so that everyone has visibility into it.*

In addition, they agree that they will make sure all PBI have a clear acceptance criteria," including testing acceptance criteria that must be satisfied. The teams decide to extend the definition of Done to put additional focus on test automation.[7]

Collaboration between teams during Sprints is greatly simplified using acceptance test-driven development. Instead of decomposing PBIs into tasks in the Sprint Backlog, state them as fine-grained acceptance tests that will drive the development of code. Tasks create opacity, and fine-grained PBIs decomposed from real PBIs retain some of the transparency.

Whenever these criteria can be evaluated through automation, the definition of "Done" will make that clear. The teams agree that they will include time to create automated tests when they estimate effort and determine their capacity.

The Product Owner also agrees that she will make more transparent when she can't be present and, if necessary, will designate someone who can represent her. She will work with those people to make sure that any decisions made reflect her vision for the Product.

Finally, the teams agree to be more realistic about progress when they take on work and to set appropriate expectations for everyone, stakeholders, and team members included.

THE CHALLENGES OF SCALING SCRUM

Nearly everyone has similar challenges when they try to scale Scrum from a single team to multiple teams working on the same Product. As more people, more teams, and more complex features are added to the mix, scaling frictions cause velocity to decline relative to the expected result (see Figure 6-5). The problem is not new, either; Fred Brooks described something similar

---

7. For more information about acceptance test-driven development, see https://en.wikipedia.org/wiki/Acceptance_test–driven_development.

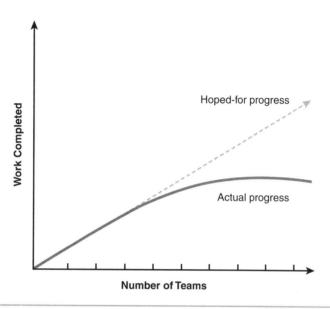

Figure 6-5 Scaling frictions can cause desired and actual results to diverge

in the mid-1970s in *The Mythical Man Month: Essays on Software Engineering.*[8]

Experiencing these challenges is normal and expected and isn't a sign that scaling is "not working," or that the teams are failing. At the same time, these challenges are not things that can be brushed aside; rather, they should be dealt with in a deliberate way. Failure to deal with these issues will eventually cause the Product, and the initiative producing it, to fail. The challenges are simply expected obstacles that nearly every organization attempting to scale Scrum should expect to encounter along the way. With Nexus, and the appropriate practices, the goal is to try to keep progress as linear as possible so that the Nexus is scalable.

---

8. From Wikipedia: "*The Mythical Man-Month: Essays on Software Engineering* is a book on software engineering and project management by Fred Brooks, whose central theme is that 'adding manpower to a late software project makes it later.' This idea is known as Brooks's law, and is presented along with the second-system effect and advocacy of prototyping." For more information, see https://en.wikipedia.org/wiki/The_Mythical_Man-Month.

Scaling product delivery, regardless whether an organization is using Scrum, another agile method, or even non-agile methods, is not a simple matter of simply adding people and teams. In order to scale effectively, organizations need to deliberately and systematically grow strong and skilled Scrum teams and detect and remove cross-team dependencies.

Adding too many people, teams, or complexity will likely lead to a decrease in productivity, if not a complete halt to progress in scaling. As a result, scaling *always* proceeds gradually. There is no magic "organizational change" program other than mindfully building practitioner skills, growing and supporting teams, and removing barriers that impede those teams from working effectively. Instead of thinking in terms of "transformation," magically going from one state to another, successful organizations scale Scrum by continuously inspecting and adapting, removing dependencies and impediments so as to improve.

CLOSING

Trust among team members and between teams and stakeholders take time to form. It is built on transparency and on demonstrated performance. Adding new people or moving people between teams erodes trust and transparency, and it takes time for teams to regain their momentum. At the same time, adding new people or moving people between teams can also bring fresh perspective and new ideas that invigorate the team.

Sometimes teams need a little help from outside to restore the balance upset by outside forces. Up until this point, the Scrum Teams in the Nexus have mostly been self-organized to deliver a working Integrated Increment, and the role of the NIT may seem relatively superfluous. In Chapter 7, "The Nexus in Emergency Mode," we will look at what happens when the Scrum Teams are not able to effectively collaborate and things spiral out of control. When this happens, the need for an NIT becomes painfully apparent.

THE NEXUS IN
EMERGENCY MODE

The true measure of any approach is how it helps people when things go badly wrong. When things are going well, nearly any approach will work. But when things start to fall apart, does the approach help teams get back on track?

The challenge in Scrum is responding to the emergency while still preserving self-organization. Telling teams what to do when things start going bad can seem expedient, but it's also demoralizing. Responding to the emergency while still empowering teams is the main challenge that the NIT faces.

> *A new Sprint brings big changes to the Nexus in the form of three new remote teams.*
>
> *The selected hardware manufacturing partner's team is in Guangzhou, China. They are nine hours offset from the rest of the Nexus located in Portland, Oregon, in the United States.*
>
> *Two of the members of the Nexus worked with the hardware vendor's team, building a proof of concept in the last Sprint. That effort went well, but having them fully integrate into the Nexus will present new challenges. Fortunately, the members of the Guangzhou team who will work on the device's firmware already have experience with Scrum.*

The bigger challenge is that the venture capital firm has found a security service provider that they think would be a good distributor/channel partner for the new product. The security service provider is currently a market leader in their industry, although they have fallen behind industry innovators. Still, they have a large customer base into which the new product could be sold. There is even the possibility of an Original Equipment Manufacturer (OEM) agreement, or potentially even an acquisition.

The security service provider has teams spread across two sites. Their web product team is in Stuttgart, Germany, and their mainframe backend team is in Bengaluru, India (see Figure 7-1). The web product team claims to already be using Scrum, but the team in Bengaluru uses a traditional "Waterfall" approach and is only making small maintenance changes. The application was moved offshore about 10 years ago and there has since been a lot of turnover on that team.

The cultural, technology, and time zone differences, coupled with the challenges of bringing together teams from three different companies, present significant challenges for the Nexus to overcome.

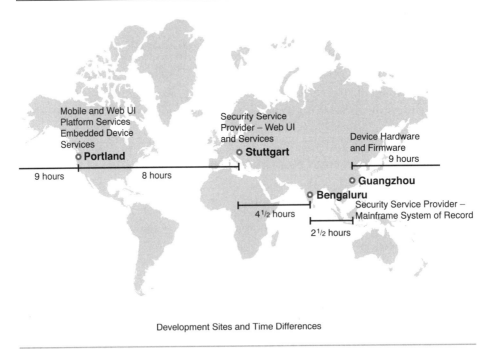

Development Sites and Time Differences

Figure 7-1 Geographically dispersed teams create a new set of collaboration challenges

PRODUCT BACKLOG REFINEMENT, TAKE THREE

Adding the new teams and focusing attention on integrating with external security systems means that the Nexus needs to further refine the Product Backlog so that the members can understand not just which teams can do what work, but also the order in which that work must be done, as well as any cross-team dependencies.

They would like to do this by bringing everyone together, but prior commitments and the time needed for processing visa applications would delay this by several weeks, so they decide to use remote collaboration technology for the refinement session.

Scrum Masters at the Stuttgart and Guangzhou locations help their teams by facilitating the session to help everyone get a chance to participate. However, the Bengaluru team is unfamiliar with Scrum, so the Scrum Master for the NIT helps the Nexus to find a local Scrum Master/trainer in Bengaluru to provide training and help to the team improve its ability to apply Scrum. Cameras in each of the team rooms, coupled with large screens and sufficient communication bandwidth to support high-quality voice and video, help to bridge the gap between sites. The main problem is that there is no good time zone and the team members in Asia end up having to work through their night, so their energy and participation levels are noticeably lower than other sites.

The Stuttgart and Bengaluru teams are also at a disadvantage since they lack the product knowledge of even the Guangzhou team. However, the Stuttgart team is familiar with customer challenges and context, and that helps. The Bengaluru team is mostly used to working from change requests and they say that they can implement whatever the other teams need, as long as the teams can help them spec out the work.

The process is imperfect but everyone feels, by the end, that the results are "good enough" to get started (see Figure 7-2).

They also update their Cross-Team Refinement Board (Figure 7-3) to include the new teams and help them understand how they all might organize their work. To share the work across sites, each team maintains its own copy of the board in its own team room. This seems very low tech, but the NIT Scrum Master insists because it will help to keep everyone engaged in creating the board if they actually have to do something with it.

Creating the board as a team uncovers two significant dependencies that will be challenging to overcome. The first is the refactoring work to create common cloud services that will help all the client application work (PBI 16). The other is adding a device to an existing security service customer account (PBI 11.2.1).

Product Backlog Items	Team	Dependencies
11 – Integrate with external security systems		
11.2 – Integrate site management features with external security service provider systems		
11.2.1 – Add doorbell to existing customer account (web)	Stuttgart	10.3
11.2.2 – Integrate with mainframe customer management & billing system	Bengaluru	11.2.1
11.2.3 – Set up device from mobile	Any Portland	11.2.1, 11.2.2
16 – Refactor common cloud services from mobile applications		
10.3 – Set up/admin device from web	Any Portland	16
2.2 – Conduct conversation with visitor through doorbell speaker using mobile device (Android)	Any Portland	16
14 – Deploy new product version		
14.1 – Deploy iOS application	Any Portland	
14.2 – Deploy Android application	Any Portland	16
14.4 – Update customer device firmware		
1.4 – Detect #doorbellRung alert event, notify web user	Any Portland	16
17 – Design and validate different hardware designs	Guangzhou	
15 – Create device/software security test automation. build into CD pipeline		
3 – View selected security camera over web or mobile device		
3.1 – Stream video using standard opensource API		
3.2 – Display streaming video on mobile device using standard opensource API		
3.3 – Display streaming video in web browser using standard opensource API		
2.3 – Conduct 2-way voice conversation via universal client API in web browser session		
8.2 – Turn off/on alerts for web client		
10.2 – Set up/admin device from mobile phone		
5 – Generate #motionDetected alert		
13 – Choose cloud platform vendor		
18 – Store + manage videos on cloud for later review		

Figure 7-2 Product Backlog, refined to reflect refactoring the mobile application and integration with the security service partner

The addition of new teams has caused the Nexus to partially revert to component teams; the Stuttgart, Guangzhou, and Bengaluru teams are organized around specific aspects of the product and, because they belong to different organizations, their parent organization's goals constrain them to only work on certain parts of the product; for example, the device manufacturer team won't be able to contribute to work on the mobile and web UIs. The Portland teams still organize around features, however.

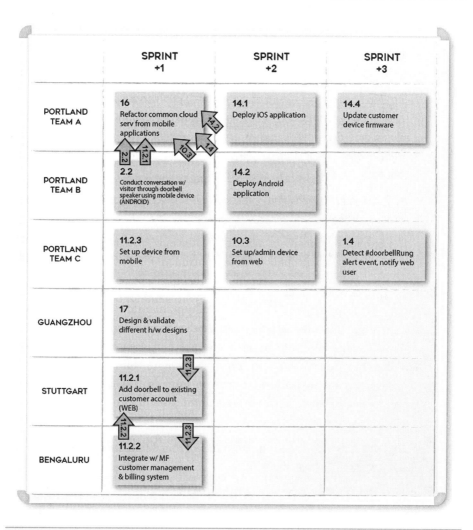

Figure 7-3 Visualizing dependencies using a Cross-Team Refinement Board

Feature teams are ideal for sharing work across teams, but they don't work in all circumstances, and a Nexus may be a mixture of component and feature teams, as is the case here.

NEXUS SPRINT PLANNING, TAKE THREE

> *Bringing the new teams into the Nexus adds capabilities and capacity but also complexity. The Product Owner would like the Nexus to focus on making sure that the product will be marketable, which means that it must be aesthetically pleasing but also sellable to the customers of the security company, a potentially large market.*
>
> *The biggest dependency the teams identified was refactoring the iOS mobile application and creating a more robust cloud service platform that all the client applications can use. The teams in Portland decide to work together on these two items until done because they are otherwise blocked and risk creating technical debt and rework if they plunge on by making assumptions. This still leaves some people with time to help other teams.*
>
> *A few members of the Portland teams also agree to help the Stuttgart team to integrate with the existing services framework, while they are waiting for the refactoring work to complete. Other Portland team members who aren't needed for the refactoring work volunteer to help the Bengaluru team create interfaces the other teams can use to access and update information that is managed by the mainframe applications.*

One of the hallmarks of an effective team, or a team of teams organized in a Nexus, is the ability of teams to flexibly organize to solve their own challenges. They don't need permission from management to do what's needed. Over time, from Sprint to Sprint, teams in a Nexus can reconfigure themselves as needed to meet their goals.

FACILITATING LARGE-SCALE DISTRIBUTED SPRINT-PLANNING SESSIONS

Large distributed meetings are difficult, and planning a Sprint is especially so. Effective Sprint planning really requires the participation of everyone in the Nexus. Distributed collaboration technology helps (e.g., webcams, virtual whiteboards, and cloud-based Sprint-planning tools) but they don't solve the fundamental problem of engaging everyone. A variety of different *diverge and merge* techniques can help them, including the following.

- **World Cafés.** Participants discuss in small groups (analogous to café tables) and circulate between groups to participate in facilitated discussions on PBIs, more deeply than they could as a large group.[1]
- **Open Spaces.** Members of the Nexus self-organize to discuss PBIs.[2]
- **Facilitators at each site.** While more of a practice than a specific technique, having someone take on a facilitation role at each location to improve engagement and participation helps to improve overall results. Most often, this will be a Scrum Master, but can be anyone if there is not a Scrum Master present at a site.

These techniques help teams to break free of their existing team structures and participate wherever their expertise is most needed. Whatever technique the teams use, Scrum Masters play an important role by making sure that everyone gets engaged and quieter voices are heard. Techniques like World Cafés and Open Spaces are designed for in-person settings, but they can be adapted to distributed environments with supporting remote collaboration technologies like Google Hangouts or similar technologies. Making these techniques work remotely, however, requires very skilled facilitators because participants will lack important in-person visual cues (e.g., facial expressions, body language).[3]

NEXUS WITH MIXED HARDWARE/SOFTWARE DEVELOPMENT

> *The Guangzhou team working on the device has relatively few constraints: They just need to prototype some new hardware designs to make sure they can meet all the functional capabilities of the earlier prototypes in a more attractive package.*

---

1. To learn more about the World Café method, see http://www.theworldcafe.com.
2. To learn more about facilitating Open Spaces, see http://openspaceworld.org/wp2/.
3. Helping distributed Scrum Teams work better together is a large and important topic on its own. For a view on how to help distributed agile teams, see https://techbeacon.com/distributed-agile-teams-8-hacks-make-them-work.

The big challenge teams face when they need to mix hardware and software development is that it can take teams vastly longer to develop hardware than it does to create software. Several techniques can be used to reduce dependencies created by these timing differences.

- **Teams can use APIs and simulation to reduce hardware dependencies.** Hardware capabilities are generally accessed through APIs. Agreeing on these APIs in early Sprints, then using simulation, also called *service virtualization*, to let developers work against and test code that calls these APIs lets teams make progress *up to a point*. The result is still working software, but it can't be shipped until the hardware dependencies are resolved. While there is a chance that the hardware can't support the APIs, or that new features will become available in later Sprints that were not in the original API specification, decoupling using APIs is a long-proven practice for mixing hardware and software development.

- **In mechanical and electronic systems, simulations can help hardware teams evaluate different designs.** Even hardware can be simulated using software, as is the case when chip design software is used to simulate how the design will work, or when mechanical engineering design applications simulate the function of parts and assemblies. These techniques have long track records in aerospace and microelectronics and can be applied in other domains as well.

- **Teams can create mechanical prototypes using 3D printing.** The rise of inexpensive 3D printing capabilities means that custom hardware designs can be prototyped in very fast cycles.

- **Electronic components can be prototyped cheaply and quickly.** Using breakout boards and fast programmable miniature computers like Arduino, teams can prototype even hardware/software integrations without the need to create specialized electrical boards.[4] Something very much like continuous integration is even possible with embedded software. An example of this is a team who created charging cradles that were capable of upgrading the device firmware overnight, as long as the device was plugged in to charge.

---

4. From Wikipedia: "Arduino is an open source computer hardware and software company, project, and user community that designs and manufactures single-board microcontrollers and microcontroller kits for building digital devices and interactive objects that can sense and control objects in the physical world." For more information, see https://en.wikipedia.org/wiki/Arduino.

As with software teams working in a Nexus, the key to improving productivity is to minimize cross-team dependencies.

TEAMS WORKING AT DIFFERENT SPRINT CADENCES

> There is some contention among the teams about Sprint boundaries and goals. The hardware and mainframe teams think that two-week Sprints are too short for them to do useful work; they would like four-week Sprints, if noy longer. The other teams feel very strongly about the value of two-week Sprints and believe that going four weeks without a working increment is too risky.

In extreme cases, it is possible for the teams in a Nexus to have different cadences, so long as the shorter cadences are evenly divisible into the longest one (see Figure 7-4). Each team must still deliver a working increment at the end of its Sprint, and it is still best if each team chooses the shortest Sprint length possible, so that the team does not go too long without delivering a working increment. The Nexus Sprint Retrospective is an ideal time for the Nexus to decide together whether it needs to change its rhythms. Nexus Sprint Planning occurs after the end of the shortest Sprint to enable the Nexus to adjust its plans as new information becomes available.

> The Bengaluru team has an additional conflict: Since it supports the existing application, which has existing customers, the team cannot devote 100% of its time to the Sprint and, as a result, the team members think that two weeks is too short a time for the Sprint.
>
> The teams reach a compromise, of sorts. The Bengaluru team will work in Sprint 3 to create a working API that will simulate the interfaces the other teams need, but they cannot implement real mainframe application access because they can't deploy new software to even their test environment due to dependencies outside their control (the mainframe test environment is shared with other applications, and the release team that manages this environment won't change their release schedule on short notice).

The Guangzhou team agrees to produce a mock-up of the new device in Sprint 3 that the stakeholders can review, but it won't have any electronics in its "guts"; that will come in a future release. The rest of the Nexus doesn't view this as a problem, so long as the interfaces to the hardware features don't change.

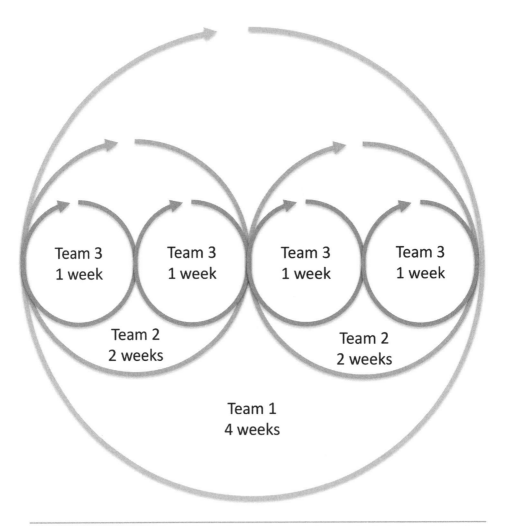

Figure 7-4 Teams can work at different Sprint cadences as long as the Sprint boundaries align

Aligning the Sprint boundaries across the Nexus helps teams to focus on delivering an *integrated* increment. Some of the teams in the case study can make partial progress in their own faster Sprint cycles, but the entire Nexus must deliver a working increment so that the organization can see whether it is making progress toward its delivery goal. If one team fails, then as a Nexus they all fail.

MIXING SCRUM AND WATERFALL APPROACHES IN A NEXUS

Mixing Waterfall and Scrum processes doesn't work; teams either follow one approach or the other, and trying to adapt Scrum to follow a milestone-driven process results in a Waterfall process with different names for events. It is possible, however, to have Scrum teams dependent on teams using a Waterfall approach if the dependencies are limited to API dependencies.

The situation is very much like that shown in Figure 7-4, with the team using the Waterfall approach having a very long delivery cycle, within which many Sprints of other teams in the Nexus will occur. Although the Integrated Increment is not shippable until the Waterfall team's delivery cycle is complete, the Scrum teams can make progress by working against APIs upon which the teams collectively agree.

The potential flaw in this approach is easy to spot: if the Waterfall team does not meet its delivery commitments, the Product Increment will not be shippable. This approach also does not allow for collaborative evolution of the APIs over a series of Sprints, as would be possible if all the teams used Scrum. It is a reasonable approach for integrating more modern products with mainframe applications, however, since the mainframe applications functionality is expected to be rather static. These mainframe applications can still evolve behind the APIs, and in fact that is a powerful strategy for application modernization.[5]

---

5. Martin Fowler describes the Strangler Application Pattern at https://www.martinfowler.com/bliki/StranglerApplication.html. Michiel Rook provides an example of how he used this to evolve a complex legacy application at https://www.michielrook.nl/2016/11/strangler-pattern-practice/.

In the case study, APIs are used to manage the dependencies on the mainframe application team, enabling other teams to make at least some progress toward their own Sprint Goals.

THE NEXUS DAILY SCRUM, TAKE THREE

As the Sprint progresses, the Nexus begins having trouble with its Nexus Daily Scrum. The team members in Bengaluru, while well-intentioned, keeps getting pulled off to deal with other production support issues, and they have difficulty with the time zone differences; their Scrum Master, who is a contractor, attends the Nexus Daily Scrum to represent the team, but he often lacks the necessary knowledge to understand and represent his team's challenges in working with the other teams. The time zone differences compound the problem, creating communication delays that make cross-team transparency more difficult.

The team in Guangzhou has a different problem: Because that team is focused on physical design issues in this Sprint, its members don't see much value in the Nexus Daily Scrum and frequently also just send their Scrum Master. This hasn't caused any problems yet, but it doesn't help to build good working relationships between teams.

The team working on refactoring the iOS application has also been struggling; the effort is turning into a rewrite and not a refactoring. Making the services general purpose enough for iOS, Android, and web clients to use is more difficult than they expected. At the same time, they have run into some technical limitations of the alerting service that need to be addressed to have a robust cross-platform service. They are discovering that some of the work they thought was "done" needs to be redone as well. This causes some churn for the Stuttgart team. They have been trying to use the web services to add a doorbell to an existing client, but the interfaces keep changing. The work on the Android client is also on hold, pending the refactoring work. As the Nexus enters the second week of the Sprint, frustration is growing.

There is also a deeper but more subtle problem: The Nexus has lost some of its cohesiveness with the addition of the new teams; they lack the singular focus on product success they once had. The "original" teams feel some resentment that they have had these newcomers forced upon them, and the new teams feel that the Nexus events are somewhat of a distraction.

The Scrum Masters from each team and the NIT's Scrum Master discuss this in one of their calls, but they are not sure what to do about it yet. They agree that it would have been better to bring all the teams together for a couple of Sprints to form a more effective extended team and to work these issues out, but the external pressure to move more quickly prevented them from doing so. Or so they tell themselves. In the meantime, they try to help their teams as best they can.

THE NEXUS DAILY SCRUM WITH DISTRIBUTED TEAMS

The Nexus Daily Scrum for distributed teams is the same as for co-located teams, but they are logistically and motivationally more challenging to support. When people don't work together every day, they tend to forget about each other, and they lapse into less transparent communication. It is easier for people to avoid talking about challenges rather than opening up and having to explain the situation to people who are not close to the issue. As a result, distributed Daily Scrum calls can become dull status reports and repetitions of "Everything is fine."

The Scrum Master for the NIT bears the responsibility for fostering transparency and helping to surface issues and broach difficult conversations. He should talk regularly to the Scrum Masters on the teams in the Nexus to understand what their teams are struggling with, so that the Scrum Masters can raise cross-team issues when the teams themselves may not feel comfortable doing so.

Because Scrum Masters for teams in the Nexus naturally talk to one another, usually daily if not more frequently, teams tend to want to delegate the attendance at the Nexus Daily Scrum to the Scrum Masters since they are talking already. This is a mistake. The Scrum Masters know enough to see the issues, but they are not always the right ones to solve each issue; the right people to better understand the issues (and who they are will vary) are the right people to attend the Nexus Daily Scrum. The "right people" will vary over time, depending on the issues.

WHAT TO DO WHEN THE NEXUS STARTS TO STRUGGLE

As everyone in the Nexus becomes more frustrated, members of all the Scrum Teams similarly start to voice that they need guidance in overcoming their challenges, and they start to look to the NIT for help. The Product Owner is becoming increasingly uncertain that the teams are making progress, and she is beginning to wonder whether the decision to add the external teams was a good one. She discusses the challenges with the investors, and they want to keep moving ahead because they feel that they need an established business partner to launch the product.

The NIT uses the Nexus Daily Scrum to understand the challenges and ask the teams what they think they need help with. The Portland and Stuttgart teams feel that the refactored services platform is their most important goal, and once they get it stabilized the work will progress more smoothly. The Bengaluru team says they just need more time to focus on the mainframe API services, but they have been pulled off to deal with other emergencies; they don't feel they have any control over this. The Guangzhou team has mocked up several design prototypes and has even tested them with the electronic "guts" of the device, so they are unaffected by the challenges of the other teams, for now.

The NIT decides to take a more active role in the work. Two of the members work with the Portland and Stuttgart teams to analyze the work to see whether it can be broken down into chunks of work that can be more easily shared across the teams. They also pitch in to develop automated tests for the services and integrate them into the continuous integration pipeline automation. This helps everyone by making sure that API regressions are discovered as soon as the developer commits code.

Another member starts working more actively with the Bengaluru team to help with developing the services that will implement the mainframe APIs, soon realizing that they will need more help to create robust API regression tests and continuous integration automation. Another member of the NIT joins in to help with this. With the NIT's help, the blockages begin to be removed.

When a Nexus is running smoothly, its teams self-organize to deliver regular releases, or at least regular demonstrations of working software. When this happens, the NIT seems largely superfluous, at best a convenient way to organize cross-team collaboration with parts of the broader world outside the Nexus.

Even this can be optional, for teams in the Nexus are certainly free to interact with whomever they need to deliver value. Like a fire warden without a fire, the NIT can seem unnecessary when things are going well. It is when things start to go wrong that the NIT's true purpose becomes abundantly clear.

ACCOUNTABILITY OF THE NIT

The NIT is accountable for ensuring that the Nexus produces an Integrated Increment at least once every Sprint. This accountability means that they are the ones who must get the Nexus back on track when things go wrong. The NIT exists to counter the natural tendency for teams to focus on their own work and leave cross-team problems for someone else to worry about. Teams that collaborate well with one another can sort out many inter-team problems by working together, but when challenges mount, they need help, and they need someone to act with authority. Making the NIT accountable for delivering an Integrated Increment gives it that authority.

THE NEXUS INTEGRATION TEAM IN EMERGENCY MODE

Taking a more active role can mean that the NIT becomes a real team with real objectives and real work to accomplish. This does not take away from the work of the Scrum teams, but augments and aids them in removing things that block their progress by taking on work on which the teams had not been able to make progress. The NIT may take on PBIs the other teams had not been able to start, or it may take work the other teams had begun but can't finish.

In emergency mode, the NIT acts just like another Scrum Team in the Nexus: It is represented at the Nexus Daily Scrum, and it has its own team Daily Scrum. At the end of the Sprint, the NIT participates in the Nexus Sprint Retrospective as a Scrum Team.

The danger lurking for the NIT in Emergency Mode is when the emergency never ends, when it is always having to step in to keep things from falling apart. When this occurs, a more complete reset of the Nexus may be needed.

DESCALING

> The venture capital firm investors are concerned that the team does not have enough resources; they put pressure on the Nexus to add more developers and testers to get more done. The NIT discusses this as an option, but they ultimately decline the offer; their problem is that they had too many people working, but ineffectively. Until the service platform and the mainframe API layer are working, adding more people will simply mean having more people waiting.
>
> They also know, from painful experience, that adding more people takes time to interview, hire, and integrate the new people into existing teams. A big part of their current problem is they have added too many people, too quickly, and they are paying the price.
>
> The investors are not completely happy with this—they are used to solving problems by simply spending money, but they decide to let the NIT try to solve the problem their way before they intrude more vigorously.

Many organizations are tempted to solve productivity problems by adding more people, but productivity issues have many causes and impediments that need to be resolved before simply adding people. The teams may lack adequate automation, they may have too many cross-team dependencies, or they may lack the right skills.

When a Nexus finds that it is not being effective, the right answer is sometimes to *descale*—to reduce the number of teams, or the size of teams, or both. In extreme cases, this might mean that going down to just a single team may be the only viable option.

It is a common mistake for organizations to assume that a particular initiative is large before they really understand the work. Sometimes this happens when they have an existing initiative that had been using a traditional approach, on which the want to try Scrum. Because they already have lots of teams, they assume that they will need lots of teams when they use Scrum.

When PBIs are too large and effort is spread across many teams, those teams will struggle to make progress because the coordination overhead will overwhelm their efforts. When teams are staffed with people who don't have the right skills, or when their skills are too narrow, they will have to involve too many people to get the work done. Scaling back to a smaller team with both broad and deep skills can often simplify delivery by removing overhead and improving focus. A paradoxical truth of modern software development is that a small, cohesive team with the right skills can make far more progress than a much larger but less focused organization.[6]

> *Having the NIT play a more active role helps, but progress is still slower than expected. The service layer refactoring work continues to take longer than expected. Not only does the Nexus need to create a robust multiplatform alerting service that accounts for offline and online notifications, they need to adapt to loss of mobile client cellular coverage. Since they hadn't adequately explored the Android and web client issues in earlier Sprints, they take some wrong turns. Pressure to integrate with the security service client portal isn't helping.*
>
> *The final straw occurs when the Bengaluru team reports that one of their team members has taken a job with another company and will be leaving the team. The team would like to make progress on the mainframe integration service layer but they are now stretched even thinner, and their other application support work hasn't diminished. The news makes the NIT realize that the Nexus is not going to reach its Sprint Goal, and continuing the current approach for another Sprint isn't going to help.*

---

6. A dramatic example of this was the FBI's Sentinel Project to produce a Virtual Case File (VCF), developed between 2000 and 2005. The project was not close to completion when it was officially abandoned in January 2005. The first two attempts at the project spent over $575 million. On the third attempt, a smaller Nexus was set up in the basement of the Hoover Building. Staff was reduced from 400 to 40, and in 1 year and spending just $30 million, they were code complete, at a cost savings of more than 90 percent. For more information, see http://www.scrumcasestudies.com/fbi/.

USING A HEALTH CHECK TO UNDERSTAND TEAM SENTIMENTS

To confirm their suspicions, and to gain new insights, the NIT Scrum Master suggests that they use a technique for understanding how teams perceive their health, something he learned from a colleague who had worked with Spotify.[7] He is concerned that if the teams feel they are not involved in the decision the NIT is about to make, they will feel even more demoralized. The NIT agrees and sees this as an opportunity to better understand the challenges they face.

The NIT has each Scrum Master lead a session with his or her team in which they consider the following aspects.

- *Are they delivering value?*
- *Is the Product easy to release?*
- *Are team members having fun?*
- *Is the Product healthy? Is it sustainable and supportable?*
- *Are team members learning?*
- *Do they understand the product goals?*
- *Do they feel like pawns or players?*
- *Is their velocity adequate?*
- *Do they feel they have a suitable process?*
- *Do they feel supported?*
- *Are they working well as a team?*

They let each team member vote on how they feel about each health indicator, then they consolidate the results (see Figure 7-5). 😊 doesn't mean everything is perfect, but the team members are at least happy with the current situation. 😐 means that there are some important problems that need to be addressed, but it's not a total disaster, and 😠 means that things are really bad and desperately need to be improved. 😟 is between 😠 and 😐, of course.

---

7. For more information on Spotify's Health Check model, see https://labs.spotify.com/2014/09/16/squad-health-check-model/.

The results largely confirm what the NIT suspected: the teams need to stop working on the Sprint Goals and need to take a step back, fix the 😟 problems, and try to make progress on the 😐 ones as well, before they move ahead. The differences between sites highlights some challenges specific teams face. That the Guangzhou team is relatively happy is not surprising because they are relatively unaffected by the refactoring and mainframe API problems.

The Bengaluru team is clearly struggling and needs more help; they feel disconnected and don't think that they are contributing or even very much involved. This is partly because they are somewhat part-time on the effort and partly because they are responsible only for a component of the solution.

The other teams are working together relatively well, though some improvements clearly need to be made.

	PDX A	PDX B	PDX C	Stuttgart	Bengaluru	Guangzhou
Delivering value	😐	😐	😐	😐	☹️	😐
Easy to release	😐	😐	😐	😐	☹️	😐
Having fun	😐	😐	😐	😐	☹️	😐
Code healthy	☹️	☹️	☹️	☹️	😐	😐
Learning	🙂	🙂	🙂	🙂	😐	🙂
Understand goals	🙂	🙂	🙂	🙂	😐	🙂
Pawns or players	🙂	🙂	🙂	😐	☹️	🙂
Velocity adequate	☹️	☹️	☹️	☹️	☹️	🙂
Suitable process	😐	😐	😐	😐	☹️	🙂
Feel supported	🙂	🙂	🙂	😐	☹️	😐
Good teamwork	🙂	🙂	🙂	😐	☹️	😐

Figure 7-5 Health Check results, summarized by team

SCRUMBLING

The purpose of Scrumbling in Nexus is an example of the old adage, "When you find yourself in a hole, stop digging." It's similar to pulling the *Andon cord* in a Lean Manufacturing approach to stop the production line.

Scrumbling helps the Nexus avoid an unpleasant surprise when it comes time to release, and it also helps to sustain transparency, reduce risk, and protect the most valuable asset—the Product—from being unacceptably degraded.

A Scrumble occurs when a Nexus cannot deliver a fully integrated, completed increment that is done and ready for use. Rather than continuing to build an unintegrated mess that becomes exponentially more difficult to fix, the Scrum teams in the Nexus Scrumble. The working team is reduced to the minimum number of people needed to deliver a working increment. The rest of the people wait and they add themselves as they are able to usefully contribute. Only when the Nexus fixes the underlying problems do they restart and resume their normal Sprint processes.

A Scrumble is not just a pause to fix a set of immediate problems. When problems accumulate to block all progress, the Nexus needs to reevaluate its way of working to understand what led it to the point of failure. A Scrumble enables the Nexus to step back from creating more problems to review and evaluate

- The effectiveness of tools and practices that are being employed to continuously or frequently integrate and deliver working Product Increment
- The effectiveness of testing strategies and execution
- The effectiveness of Product Backlog decomposition, ordering, and selection
- The effectiveness of Sprint Backlog management practices
- The value of common development and testing tools and platforms that help teams focus on meeting their Sprint Goals
- The adequacy of continuous delivery practices in helping the teams deliver an integrated increment, that meets both functional and nonfunctional requirements, every Sprint
- Strategies and execution of branching and integration practices

Actions the Nexus may take to resolve issues identified include

- Upgrading the development environment and practices
- Remediating and refactoring existing code to make it more maintainable, extensible, and testable

- Creating a comprehensive set of automated regression tests
- Creating a usable, reviewable integrated increment
- Creating development and test environments that support the teams
- Training the developers in practices that use the development environment
- Developing system-specific tools and components to reduce dependencies
- The Product Owner working with customers, investors, and other stakeholders to redefine goals and expectations for the upcoming Product launches

Once the Scrumble is complete, the Nexus should be better prepared to deliver usable increments. The next Sprint can then begin.

The length of time needed for a Scrumble varies with the skills, environment, people, and existing software, but the duration of at least one Sprint should be expected; when the problems are serious enough to stop all work, the Nexus will need time to address the root causes. One Scrumble may be enough, but if the Nexus again finds itself with unreleasable/undone increments, it may need to Scrumble again.[8]

After deciding that they need to stop, step back, reassess, and rework, the Nexus arrives at the following solution: The Stuttgart team, except for one developer and their Scrum Master, will take a break and work on maintenance work for their existing system. All work on web and mobile clients will stop until the web services are refactored; the development teams know enough to do the work, and those who are not working on refactoring will help them by writing a robust set of regression tests for the framework. In the process, they will fine-tune the continuous integration pipeline, as well as clean up some problems in the source code repository created by a feature-branching misstep made in an earlier Sprint.

To solve the mainframe integration problem, three developers from Portland who have worked on the refactored service platform will work remotely with the Bengaluru developers to create services that will provide the mainframe

---

8. If this were to occur, the people paying for the Product to be developed may lose faith in what the teams. This possibility makes it even more important that Scrumbling addresses the root causes of the difficulties the Nexus is experiencing.

application integration APIs. With the local team's help, they think they can develop a working service layer in a few weeks, even if the local developers get pulled off to work on something else. They can start the work remotely and then, in a few weeks when they have visas, they can finish the work in person.

THE NEXUS (PSEUDO) SPRINT REVIEW AND RETROSPECTIVE

It takes the Nexus three weeks to stabilize the service platform, including creating robust automated regression tests so a developer will know immediately if they have broken something upon which others depend. They can finally stop Scrumbling. The mainframe interface work finishes faster; once they have the right people, who understand both the mainframe application and how to build modern services, working closely together, they create a stable set of APIs, including automated regression tests.

In addition, the teams finally have time to streamline the continuous integration automation and build comprehensive automated API-based tests that execute every time code is committed. This gives them a lot of confidence that the integration problems they had been experiencing will be resolved more easily. The Product Owner's confidence that the Product is back on track significantly improves, and she shares this with the investors.

To better understand how the teams are feeling, the Scrum Masters conduct another Health Check. This time the results are significantly better (see Figure 7-6). The Stuttgart and Bengaluru teams still feel somewhat disconnected, and although the immediate roadblocks have been removed there is still much that needs to be improved. The most important thing is that everyone feels less frustrated and is looking forward to getting started on the next Sprint.

The remaining challenges for the Bengaluru team are that they are only responsible for the mainframe component, and they are often pulled to work on other things. They see the benefits of working on feature teams and would like to have the opportunity, but their other responsibilities, dictated by their management, prevent them from taking a broader role in the Nexus.

	PDX A	PDX B	PDX C	Stuttgart	Bengaluru	Guangzhou
Delivering value	😊	😊	😊	😊	😞	😊
Easy to release	😊	😊	😊	🙂	😞	😊
Having fun	😊	😊	😊	🙂	😞	😊
Code healthy	😊	😊	😊	🙂	🙂	😊
Learning	😊	😊	😊	😊	😐	😊
Understand goals	😊	😊	😊	😊	🙂	😊
Pawns or players	😊	😊	😊	🙂	😞	😊
Velocity adequate	😊	😊	😊	😞	😞	😊
Suitable process	😊	😊	😊	🙂	😞	😊
Feel supported	😊	😊	😊	😐	😞	🙂
Good teamwork	😊	😊	😊	🙂	😞	🙂

Figure 7-6 Health Check results, after Scrumbling, summarized by team

CLOSING

The true test of a team, and its approach to Product delivery, is how its members respond to crises. When the Nexus encounters a crisis to which the Scrum Teams are unable to respond, the NIT has to take action to help the Scrum teams respond, learn, and adapt. Scrumbling takes this even further, by suspending normal work until the crisis is resolved and the root causes of the crisis are addressed.

Nexus is an approach that enables a team of Scrum Teams to deliver large, complex Products. But Nexus has a limit of approximately nine Scrum teams; beyond that, coordination complexity and cross-team dependencies grow too large for the mechanisms of Nexus alone to respond.

In the next and final chapter, we will use a retrospective approach to review and reflect on the challenges that Nexus helps Scrum Teams to meet.

RETROSPECTIVE ON THE NEXUS JOURNEY

> *Several months and many Sprints pass. The crisis that resulted in the Scrumble is a distant memory, and the Nexus delivers its first release to the market. The teams are happy with the result and, significantly, so are the investors. The Nexus has delivered a product that customers love, and though there is still much to improve, the revenues have been strong enough to continue improving the product.*
>
> *With the release behind them, the Scrum Masters in the Nexus suggest to the teams that it might be a good idea if they all did a retrospective on the whole release. This would allow them to take a step back to look at the entire journey they have been on since they came together as a Nexus. The teams agree that it might help them understand what they could do better for the next release.*

As you already know by now, the Nexus Sprint Retrospective is the primary way a Nexus reflects upon and improves the way it is working. Normally the scope for this is the most recent Sprint, but it's sometimes useful to look across Sprints for trends or common challenges. When the teams in a Nexus release their product in a Sprint, it feels natural for them, though not mandatory, to look across the span of the release to spot any trends they missed during previous retrospectives.

WHAT WORKED WELL

> *The results from the Retrospective confirmed some things the teams already knew and highlighted some interesting benefits they had overlooked before.*

THE NEXUS DAILY SCRUM

> *There were a lot of positive mentions for the Nexus Daily Scrum. The team members who had used the Scrum of Scrums technique before believed that meeting first as a Nexus before the teams did their own Daily Scrums helped them to resolve integration issues faster. They thought the small amount of additional structure didn't get in the way and actually surfaced issues faster, saving them lots of time in the long run.*

Nexus enables teams to use inspection and adaptation, supported by transparency, to not only foster a better way of working but ultimately to deliver better results. As time passes, after they have worked together for a long time, they can become complacent and slip into bad habits such as letting the Nexus Daily Scrum turn into a status reporting meeting or having Scrum Teams skip the Nexus Daily Scrum entirely. The Nexus Scrum Master needs to help the Nexus keep the meeting meaningful by making sure that cross-team issues are raised in the Nexus Daily Scrum.

The Nexus Daily Scrum is an opportunity for the Nexus to provide a transparent view of how integration for the increment is working and to give a formal opportunity to identify any issues that need resolving as the teams plan their work for the day. It focuses on identifying integration challenges. Following the Nexus Daily Scrum with the individual team Daily Scrums helps the teams address the cross-team challenges, not just their own.

THE NEXUS INTEGRATION TEAM

> *Another positive item cited by many team members is the role of the NIT. One team member highlights that he did not see the value of having a separate team, but after seeing how the NIT worked when the Nexus was in emergency mode, he now fully understands why having such a team is valuable.*

Scrum relies upon self-organization to help teams accomplish their work in order to deliver solutions, but adds just enough structure to make sure that things don't get forgotten. The key to this is accountability: While teams can be jointly responsible for delivering solutions, team members in specific roles are *accountable* for the results.

In Scrum, the Product Owner is *accountable* for the Product. In Nexus, the NIT (which includes the Product Owner) is accountable for ensuring an *integrated* Product is produced at least every Sprint. Because the NIT is ideally composed of members from each of the individual Scrum Teams, all voices can be heard, encouraging bottom-up intelligence to help resolve issues.

There is a balance between the accountability and bottom-up intelligence: The Product Owner needs the bottom-up intelligence provided by releases to know that the Product is solving the right problems and delivering the right value. The NIT needs bottom-up intelligence to know what is working, and more important, what is not working, so that they can help the Scrum Teams improve their technical excellence through coaching or other enabling work.

Ideally, Scrum Teams would self-organize to solve all their problems, but sometimes they cannot see the cross-team problems well enough to resolve them. In our case study, the Scrum Teams were so close to the growing integration problem that no one of them could make the call to bring development to a halt until the fundamental technical debt and mainframe integration issues were resolved. Holding the NIT accountable for having an integrated Product also gave it the *authority* to decide to halt normal development until the integration blockers were resolved. In addition, the Product Owner (part of the NIT as well), lent her authority to the decision to Scrumble until the blocking issues were resolved.

RELEASE FREQUENCY

> *Over the course of the release, the Scrum Teams used their own need to update any part of the product at any time into a continuous delivery capability; they were now able to release new versions of device firmware, mobile applications, web applications, and web services any time they needed to, at the Product Owner's discretion.*
>
> *They discussed whether they still needed the Nexus Sprint Review since they were releasing all the time. The Product Owner decided that she still needed the Nexus Sprint Review to periodically bring stakeholders together to provide feedback on the integrated Product. With software releasing every day, it was useful to be able to step back and look at what they had accomplished over the course of the Sprint.*

The Nexus Sprint Review is not a release decision gate. The Nexus can release anytime its Product Owner thinks the product is ready to release, which might very well be many times a day. In these circumstances, the Nexus Sprint Review is still important as an opportunity for the Nexus and its stakeholders to step back and consider how the product is progressing towards its goals. This is more important, not less, as a team's release frequency increases: When teams are releasing all the time, progress toward product goals can get lost in the flurry of constant release activity.

A Sprint is a time box that manages the planning, building, and reviewing cycle of the team, not the release. The length of a Sprint for a Nexus is determined by the constraints of the teams and stakeholders and the complexity of the problem being solved, not the technology being used. For example, if key stakeholders cannot provide feedback on the product every week, then the Sprint should be longer. If the work lends itself to larger goals, then the Sprint should be longer. If the team likes a shorter or longer rhythm, then the Sprint should be constrained to fit those needs. It is, however, important to keep the Sprint cadence regular and short enough to encourage focus and action without being burdensome and considered by the team to get in the way of work. And, the best Nexus Sprint Reviews are performed with real data, from real customers, using the software in production.

PRODUCTIVITY

> *The Scrum Teams also thought they got a lot done, more than they expected to when they first formed the Nexus. The release was a significant accomplishment, and they had enough experience with other approaches. The Scrumble was a big part of this, as they recognized, in retrospect, that they needed to stop and resolve their fundamental challenges before they could make progress.*
>
> *They also found that the Nexus Daily Scrum helped them to deal with cross-team challenges as they came up. It made it easier to get a couple of people from the different Scrum Teams together to resolve an issue when it happened; without that and a focus on the Nexus Goal, they felt they might have let things slide while they focused on their own work. The Nexus Goal also helped them build and maintain an identity as a Nexus.*

The joy of getting things done, together, is the best motivation a team can experience. Team morale often tracks along with accomplishments; when everyone feels productive, and when they are not held back by impediments, they are happier and feel more invested in what they are producing. Conversely, when obstacles arise and are not quickly removed, morale and motivation suffer.

SELF-ORGANIZATION

> *Self-organization was highlighted as a key difference that improved the way the Nexus performed. The teams discussed how this not only allowed the people with the knowledge of the situation take control of how they worked, but also meant that everyone felt they had ownership of the solution. This motivated the team. One team member went so far as to say, "The inmates are now running the asylum—and it feels good."*

The idea of self-organization is fundamental to Agile, and its power was identified in a pivotal paper that shaped Scrum: "The New New Product

Development Game."[1] In this paper, the authors identify that one of the key characteristics of successful innovative organizations is the ability of the teams to organize and reorganize based on the situation. However, in most large companies, teams are formed by "management," usually based on complex HR, Finance, and PMO planning. The larger the organization, the more disconnected the planning process is from the people being moved. Self-organization is a fundamental tenant for Nexus, allowing the teams to inspect and adapt based on the situation. This people-empowered approach can challenge many traditional organizational constructs but allows teams to form based on their changing knowledge of the situation.

> *Several of the more technical team members also highlighted the value of solid engineering practice. They talked about release automation and the continuous integration process. However, many members of the team said that the level of automation was never enough, and they could have started earlier.*

Building robust, reliable software requires more than just teams working well together. They must also use solid engineering practices. Practices like continuous integration, or even continuous delivery, help them to be more consistent and effective. Keeping technical debt small is equally important, if not more so, because when it is not managed it can quickly grow until it threatens the viability of the product. Just as inspection and adaptation help teams to build the right solution, they also help teams to build the solution right by exposing problems early, provided that the teams don't ignore the signals. Transparency about issues helps the Product Owner make the right decisions concerning focus and priority.

AREAS FOR IMPROVEMENT

Areas for improvement include managing technical debt, scaling the product owner, developing skills, and establishing transparency and trust.

---

1. "The New New Product Development Game" can be found at https://hbr.org/1986/01/the-new-new-product-development-game.

Managing Technical Debt

> *There was a lot of discussion about how the teams felt they could have better managed technical debt earlier. In retrospect, they realized that having better build and test automation, earlier, and investing in the services framework earlier rather than putting too much effort into the iOS app, would have made things better in the long run. At the time, they felt that making progress on features was more important, but they realized that doing so hurt their productivity later.*
>
> *There was some discussion about the Product Owner's role in this; she realized that in pushing for features over dealing with technical debt she didn't fully understand the benefits of reducing technical debt. Having witnessed the problems that led to the Scrumble, she felt she had a greater appreciation of the contribution of both architecture and automation toward a great Product.*

Just like with the mythical man-month[2] and the silver bullet,[3] there is no such thing as a perfect product. Because software is only constrained by a person's imagination, the number of things that can be added or changed is almost infinite. The friction between architectural concerns such as maintainability, security, performance, and adaptability and the immediate needs of quality, and new customer-driven features makes for a healthy product.

The ultimate arbiter of this dilemma is the Product Owner, who is responsible for ordering the Product Backlog to maximize value of the product. To enable the Product Owner to make informed decisions, changes driven by the concerns of the architecture must be communicated in the same way as new features. There is no "technical magic" card that can be played. Instead, the Product Backlog provides a transparent view of ALL the work, which includes technical debt, defects, and new customer features.

---

2. Few books have captured the issues of software engineering better than Fred Brooks's classic work, *The Mythical Man-Month: Essays on Software Engineering*. This book describes the fallacy of thinking that software projects can be treated in the same way as traditional engineering projects, where work will be reduced by the addition of people.
3. "No Silver Bullet—Essence and Accident in Software Engineering" is a widely discussed paper by Fred Brooks on the characteristics of software projects available at http://worrydream.com/refs/Brooks-NoSilverBullet.pdf.

To help teams tackle this problem, some organizations introduce guard rails into the planning process that provide guidance for the percentage of work in each area. For example, you may decide that for the next three Sprints you tackle 70 percent customer features and 30 percent technical debt (including fixing defects). These guard rails provide a vision for the product and reduce the debate in Nexus Sprint Planning. They are, however, just guidelines and don't replace the Product Owner's right to decide what is the most valuable work. Guard rails don't diminish the need to build great software every Sprint by setting aside some time to reduce technical debt; the guidelines simply remind the teams that poor-quality software can never be great, and that they need to invest, in every Sprint, in keeping the code clean.

SCALING THE PRODUCT OWNER

The Product Owner recognized that she had had trouble providing all the support the Scrum Teams needed, particularly the teams in remote locations. Scrum Team members stepped up to represent her as best they could when she was not available, but some issues lingered for a while before she had time to deal with them.

Going forward, they agreed that the Scrum Teams would designate delegates for the Product Owner for the remote teams. These delegates would still develop, but their first responsibility would be to help to represent the Product Owner, and the amount of work they would pull from the Product Backlog would reflect this.

Working with lots of Scrum Teams can be a challenge for the Product Owner. Nevertheless, having a single voice of authority on Product decisions is essential. When a single Product Owner can't be everywhere at once, or cannot interact with all the teams when they need guidance, she can designate other team members to represent her.

This does not mean that there are multiple "levels" of Product Ownership (such as a "Chief Product Owner" and "Subordinate Product Owners," potentially organized into a Product Owner team, or, even worse, different

Product Owners for different Features).[4] There still needs to be one Product Owner to make the critical decisions about the product, but she can enlist the help of others to represent her when she can't be present all the time.

SKILL DEVELOPMENT

> *Nearly everyone liked the rotating of people through different Scrum Teams but thought that knowledge was still not being effectively communicated outside of the teams. One team member highlighted the amount of time they wasted on building a test harness that was described in the following Nexus Sprint Review as "just like mine" by a member of another team.*

Nexus provides mechanisms to help teams focus on building great software, but organizations may need more to share broader information across teams. Unless they happen to have an informal conversation about what they are working on, team members on different teams may not know what each other is working on until the Nexus Sprint Review. When this leads to duplicated effort, people can become frustrated.

Communities of practice provide a mechanism for sharing practices and experience across an organization. They utilize a variety of different techniques, from discussion groups, hangouts, or periodic presentations sharing successes and challenges between peers. Successful communities of practice often require some level of leadership, either in the form of a dedicated steward or a group of stewards who take responsibility for the area. Communities can form around roles such as Scrum Master or Product Owner, technologies such as Ruby or Python, or disciplines such as test automation, data analytics, or design. They can also form around business domains such as claims processing or customer acquisition. They answer the need of people in different teams to share experiences with their peers across the organization.

---

4. A better solution may be to have different Product Owners for different personas, but before doing this, ask the question whether the Product should be broken into more than one Product, one per persona. Having separate Products for different personas makes releases smaller and simpler, unless the personas must interact to fulfill specific outcomes. In that case, addressing their interrelated needs with one Product is still best.

TRANSPARENCY AND TRUST

> There were several items about how team members did not feel able to share problems in a transparent way. In fact, one team member went as far as to say, "When I was working on the backend stuff with the backend team, I felt comfortable to tell the team when I felt there was a problem. When we reorganized to our customer teams, I was the only person in the team that knew anything about the back end, so I did not feel comfortable sharing my issues with my new team. I mean, I had just joined them and did not want to make it sound like it was a mistake me being there."

One benefit and challenge with the Nexus is that teams can reform based on the whole team's knowledge of the current situation. This is a great way to foster self-organization and agility, but can undermine the feeling of safety provided by a team. The Nexus is a social system and populated not by robots but by people.

Scrum accepts this reality and provides the values of Courage, Focus, Commitment, Respect, and Openness to foster an environment of transparency and dialogue (see Figure 8-1)[5]. Unfortunately, the description of the values in itself does not make them a reality in a Nexus, and it is often left to the Scrum Master(s) to remind the team of these values and encourage behavior that supports them. To scale the values within an organization requires them to be followed not only by the Scrum Teams but also by the people outside of the Scrum Teams. Leadership, HR, help desks, and all the supporting roles within an organization also need to follow these values.

One technique to encourage people to follow these values is to put a poster with them on the wall and then call out any example behaviors at the Nexus Sprint Retrospective. Some teams add funny prizes for team members that have gone above and beyond in demonstrating a value, like a toy lion is given to the last person that demonstrated courage.

---

5. For more about the values behind Scrum, see https://www.scrum.org/resources/blog/updates-scrum-guide-5-scrum-values-take-center-stage.

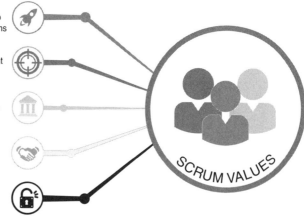

Courage
Scrum Team members have courage to do the right thing and work on though problems

Focus
Everyone focuses on the work of the Sprint and the goals of the Scrum Team

Commitment
People personally commit to achieving the goals of the Scrum Team

Respect
Scrum Team members respect each other to be capable, independent people

Openness
The Scrum Team and its stakeholders agree to be open about all the work and the challenges with performing the work

Figure 8-1 Scrum Values

SCRUM VALUES

Nexus, like Scrum, is NOT a methodology dictating the detailed activities of the organization throughout the endeavor. Instead, Nexus provides a framework with a few simple rules, artifacts, roles, and events that help the teams discover the right process for their specific problem.

Nexus will not solve an organization's problems, but if applied correctly will make sure those problems are positioned to be solved. However, the power of Nexus can be undermined by a culture where inspection, adaption, transparency, and improvement are less important than ignoring problems, which allows no ability to change and which hides the issues. Culture, unfortunately, is the hardest thing to change, and this can undermine any transformation. Nexus and Scrum cannot solve the problems of culture, but the Scrum Guide provides some help with the definition of five values (see Table 8-1).

These values guide how teams work and where they can improve. The values are Commitment, Focus, Openness, Respect, and Courage. Each value provides an ethical perspective on how Scrum and Nexus works.

Table 8-1 The Five Values

Value	Definition
Commitment	Perhaps the easiest value to confuse with the desire by management to "commit" to an outcome of a Sprint. But commitment is addressing the commitment by the team to following Nexus and Scrum. A commitment to the people in the Nexus and Scrum Teams. The teams' dedication to the work, and not a commitment to any particular outcome other than learning.
Focus	The Sprint provides a clear time box that allows the team to focus on the goal of the Sprint and not be distracted by other matters. Focus also describes the idea in Scrum and Nexus to do the least necessary to deliver the value described in the goal and the associated backlog items.
Openness	Traditional industrial processes often encouraged a culture of subterfuge where honesty and openness were weak, and problems were not considered to be an issue if you could blame someone else. Scrum and Nexus require a different approach where transparency is encouraged to enable the team to adapt. Without transparency, Scrum fails to work as the team can adapt to issues and reality is not considered. Openness also encourages openness across the Nexus, with teams collaborating, sharing knowledge, and maybe reorganizing in response to the situation.
Respect	A Nexus comprises many different people with different experiences and skills. It is important that respect is shown for everyone, even if those people approach things from a different viewpoint. Traditionally, management was expected to ensure that everyone is contributing. With Nexus and Scrum, this responsibility is held by everyone. Respect encourages everyone to contribute because it provides the idea that everyone's ideas are safe from insult or ridicule.
Courage	In support of respect, courage leads to an environment where everyone is empowered to contribute and to challenge the team or their own situation. This value is best manifested in a product that customers want and a delivery process that is rewarding for the team.

WHAT'S NEXT?

Based on their Retrospective, the teams create an enterprise improvement backlog, which they will use to guide their efforts to improve their delivery capabilities. These include experimenting with a community of practice for developers to share information across teams. Everyone seems happy that they took the time to step

> *back from the day-to-day work to focus on what had worked well from day one and what they could learn from. Then, the rhythm of the Nexus took over and they kicked off the Nexus Sprint Planning event for the next Sprint. The Product Owner started with "That was a great Sprint. Now we really need to focus on...."*

Delivering amazing products that wow customers is actually a very simple process. You have an idea, create a hypothesis, build something to evaluate that hypothesis, test it, review your findings, and start again.[6] But, without transparency across the customer, owners, builders, leaders, and other stakeholders, this very simple process can get easily broken.

As you add people, lose site of the customer and your mission, and use technology that is unproven or technology that has massive technical debt, it is easy to start thinking that the answer is more up-front planning, more process, more roles, more events, and more detailed schedules. Doing so creates a fog of activity that creates an illusion that more work is getting done, when the reality is that less value is being delivered.

The reality is that the path to sustainable business agility is to focus on building high-performing teams, reducing dependencies between those teams, and removing constraints and inhibitors.

And what works in small scale can work in the large, to a point. Teams can grow to 7±2 members, and a Nexus can grow to 7±2 teams. Multiple Nexuses are possible. Beyond that, the overhead of ensuring transparency and the challenge of maintaining the benefits of self-organization require solid modular architectures, isolation of concerns, and extensive automation to allow you to stay small, focused, and agile.

CLOSING

As we said at the beginning, scaled Scrum is still Scrum, and so Nexus is still Scrum; a little bit has been added to help reduce or eliminate cross-team dependencies and to maintain transparency, but it's still Scrum.

---

6. A great overview for the new paradigm to business can be found in *Sense and Respond: How Successful Organizations Listen to Customers and Create New Products Continuously* by Jeff Gothelf and Josh Seiden.

To scale effectively, you need to master the basics. The good news is that if you're already using Scrum, you've got an excellent foundation.

We've tried to show in the case study that teams don't have to be perfect to use Nexus, but they do have to be diligent. They still need to inspect and adapt their own practices, and they need to earnestly seek to improve their performance. This isn't always easy, but the struggle is part of the journey.

When you run into difficulties, go back to the Scrum Values to look for ways to improve. We have found that they provide teams with a way to frame the improvement discussions to challenge themselves to do better.

We also left a couple of important values off the list of Scrum Values because we hope you can apply them in everything you do. Have fun! Enjoy working together to build cool things that people love, and keep your sense of humor! It really helps when the going gets tough to be able to step back and laugh about it, even just a little.

Good luck!

WHERE TO LEARN MORE

Scrum.org continues to invest in and evolve Nexus. The definitive online guide to Nexus can be found at https://www.scrum.org/resources/online-nexus-guide.

This book on Nexus is the first in a series about Professional Scrum. Future titles in the series will cover various roles within Scrum, including the Product Owner.

Nexus case studies and more information about how to scale Scrum can be found at https://www.scrum.org/resources/scaling-scrum.

Finally, the Scrum.org community blog contains a wealth of topics related to applying and scaling Scrum: https://www.scrum.org/resources/blog.

Good luck, and Scrum On!

—Kurt, Patricia, and Dave

GLOSSARY

A

Application Lifecycle Management (ALM)   A holistic view on the management of software applications and systems, accounting for all stages of the existence of a software product, from idea through build, test, deployment, and end of life.

Acceptance Test-Driven Development (ATDD)   A test-first software development practice in which acceptance criteria for new functionality are created as automated tests. The failing tests are constructed to pass as development proceeds and acceptance criteria are met.

B

Behavior-Driven Development (BDD)   An agile software development practice adding to TDD the description of the desired functional behavior of the new functionality. BDD usually includes what is called "executable specifications." Tests written in plain text that can be executed automatically.

Branching   A source code management technique that creates a logical or physical copy of code within a version control system so that this copy might be changed in isolation.

Burn-down Chart A chart showing the evolution of remaining effort against time. Burn-down charts are an optional implementation within Scrum to make progress transparent.

Burn-up Chart A chart showing the evolution of an increase in a measure, such as Story Points or number of Product Backlog Items, against time. Burn-up charts are an optional implementation within Scrum to make progress transparent.

C

Clean Code An attribute of source code that is expressed well, formatted correctly, and organized for later coders to understand. Clarity is preferred over cleverness.

Code Coverage A measurement indicating the amount of product code that is exercised by tests.

Cohesion and Coupling Coupling is a measure of how interdependent a set of modules are, whereas cohesion is a measure of how related the functions within a single module are. The goal is to achieve strong cohesion while having low coupling.

Collective Code Ownership A software development principle popularized by Extreme Programming, holding that all contributors to a given code base are jointly responsible for the code in its entirety.

Continuous Delivery A software delivery practice similar to continuous deployment except a human action is required to promote changes into a subsequent environment along the pipeline.

Continuous Deployment A software delivery practice in which the release process is fully automated in order to have changes promoted to the production environment with no human intervention. This approach requires very strong automated quality processes throughout the deployment pipeline.

Continuous Integration (CI) An agile software development practice popularized by Extreme Programming in which newly checked-in code is built, integrated, and tested frequently, generally multiple times a day.

Cyclomatic Complexity   A measure of code complexity based on the number of independent logical paths through a method or function. Cyclomatic complexity is expressed as a simple integer.

Cross-functional   A characteristic of a team that possesses all the skills required to successfully produce a releasable Increment in a Sprint.

D

Daily Scrum   A daily time-boxed event of 15 minutes or less during which the Development Team replans the next day of development work during a Sprint. Decisions are reflected as updates to the Sprint Backlog.

Definition of Done   A shared understanding of expectations that the Increment must live up to in order to be releasable into production. Managed by the Development Team.

Developer   Any member of a Development Team, regardless of technical, functional, or other specialty.

DevOps   An organizational concept bridging the gap between development and operations, in terms of skills, mind-set, practices, and silo mentality. The underlying idea is that developers are aware of—and in daily work consider implications on—operations, and vice versa.

Development Team   The role within a Scrum Team accountable for managing, organizing, and doing all development work required to create a releasable Increment of Product every Sprint.

E

Emergence   The process of the coming into existence or prominence of new facts or new knowledge of a fact, or knowledge of a fact becoming visible unexpectedly.

Empiricism   A process control type in which only the past is accepted as certain and in which decisions are based on observation, experience, and experimentation. Empiricism has three pillars: transparency, inspection, and adaptation.

Engineering Standards   A shared set of development and technology standards that a Development Team applies to create releasable Increments of software.

F

Feature Toggle   A software development practice that allows dynamically turning (parts of) functionality on and off without impacting the overall accessibility of the system by its users.

Forecast (of Functionality)   The selection of items from the Product Backlog a Development Team deems feasible for implementation in a time period, such as a Sprint or Release cycle.

I

Increment   The latest working version of a Product, which in turn builds upon previously created Increments. Building a Product incrementally means that the Product grows larger with each increment.

Integrated Increment   The Increment of functionality created by all Scrum Teams during the Sprint. The definition of "Done" is shared across multiple Scrum Teams.

N

Nexus   A framework that extends Scrum to enable multiple Scrum Teams to use a single Product Backlog to deliver an integrated Product. It enables organizations to apply Scrum's iterative and incremental approach to Product delivery to deliver large, complex Products.

Nexus Daily Scrum   A daily planning meeting in which the representatives from the Scrum Teams in a Nexus discuss cross-team dependencies and integration challenges before the Daily Scrum of each Scrum Team.

Nexus Integration Team (NIT)   A Scrum Team who is accountable for the Nexus producing a fully Integrated Increment at least every Sprint, and whose primary work is to coordinate and guide the work of the Nexus Scrum Teams. The Integration Team consists of a Scrum Master, Product Owner, and people with other necessary skills. Nexus Integration Team members may be virtual or members of other Scrum teams, provided that their Nexus Integration Team responsibilities take precedence.

Nexus Sprint Backlog   A high-level plan that coordinates work for all Scrum Teams within a Nexus, highlighting dependencies between teams and among Product Backlog Items.

Nexus Sprint Planning   An event that creates a plan for an upcoming Sprint for all Scrum Teams within a Nexus. This meeting is structured to wring out dependencies, enable coordinated work, and deliver an integrated Increment.

Nexus Sprint Review   An event that coordinates overall progress by inspecting the integrated Increment and making appropriate adaptations to future planned work.

Nexus Sprint Retrospective   An event during which the Nexus Integration Team and representatives from the Scrum Teams of the Nexus evaluate and improve how the Nexus operates.

P

Pair Programming   An agile software development practice popularized by Extreme Programming in which two team members jointly create new functionality.

Product Backlog   An ordered list of the work to be done to create, maintain, and sustain a product. Managed by the Product Owner.

Product Backlog Refinement   The activity in a Sprint through which the Product Owner and the Development Team add granularity to the Product Backlog and enhance common understanding about the Product Backlog Items.

Product Owner   The role in Scrum accountable for maximizing the value of a product, primarily by incrementally managing and expressing business and functional expectations for a product to the Development Team(s).

R

Ready   A shared understanding by the Product Owner and the Development Team regarding the preferred level of description and granularity of Product Backlog Items introduced at Sprint Planning.

Refactoring   An agile software development practice popularized by Extreme Programming in which code is improved within the code base without impacting the external, functional behavior of that code.

S

Scrum A framework to support teams in complex product development. Scrum consists of Scrum Teams and their associated roles, events, artifacts, and rules, as defined in the Scrum Guide.

Scrum Board A physical board to visualize information for and by the Scrum Team, often used to manage Sprint Backlog. Scrum boards are an optional implementation within Scrum to make information visible.

Scrum Guide The definition of Scrum, written and provided by Ken Schwaber and Jeff Sutherland, co-creators of Scrum. This definition consists of Scrum's roles, events, and artifacts, as well as the rules that bind them together.

Scrum Master The role within a Scrum Team accountable for guiding, coaching, teaching, and assisting a Scrum Team and its environments in a proper understanding and use of Scrum.

Scrum Team A self-organizing team consisting of a Product Owner, Development Team, and Scrum Master.

Scrum Values A set of fundamental values and qualities underpinning the Scrum framework: commitment, focus, openness, respect, and courage. When these values are embodied and lived by the Scrum Team, the Scrum pillars of transparency, inspection, and adaptation come to life and build trust for everyone. The Scrum Team members learn and explore those values as they work with the Scrum events, roles, and artifacts.

Self-organization The management principle that teams autonomously organize their work. Self-organization happens within boundaries and against given goals. Teams choose how best to accomplish their work rather than being directed by others outside the team.

Sprint A time-boxed event of 30 days or less that serves as a container for the other Scrum events and activities. Sprints are done consecutively, without intermediate gaps.

Sprint Backlog An overview of the development work to realize a Sprint's goal, typically a forecast of functionality and the work needed to deliver that functionality. Managed by the Development Team.

Sprint Goal   A short expression of the purpose of a Sprint, often a problem that is addressed. Functional scope might be adjusted durﬁ Sprint in order to achieve the Sprint Goal.

Sprint Planning   A time-boxed event of 8 hours or less, used to start a Sprint. It allows the Scrum Team to inspect the work from the Product Backlog that's most valuable to be done next and design that work into a Sprint backlog.

Sprint Retrospective   A time-boxed event of 3 hours or less, ending a Sprint. It is used by the Scrum Team to inspect the past Sprint and plan for improvements to be enacted during the next Sprint.

Sprint Review   A time-boxed event of 4 hours or less, concluding the development work of a Sprint. It serves for the Scrum Team and the stakeholders to inspect the Increment of product resulting from the Sprint, assess the impact of the work performed on overall progress, and update the Product backlog to maximize the value of the next period.

Stakeholder   A person external to the Scrum Team with a specific interest in and knowledge of a product that is required for incremental discovery. Represented by the Product Owner and actively engaged with the Scrum Team at Sprint Review.

T

Test-Driven Development (TDD)   A test-first software development practice in which test cases are defined and created first, and subsequently executable code is created to make the test pass. The failing tests are constructed to pass as development proceeds and tests succeed.

Technical Debt   The typically unpredictable overhead of maintaining the product, often caused by less than ideal design decisions, contributing to the total cost of ownership. May exist unintentionally in the Increment or introduced purposefully to realize value earlier.

U

User Story   An agile software development practice from Extreme Programming to express requirements from an end-user perspective, emphasizing verbal communication. In Scrum, it is often used to express functional items on the Product Backlog.

Unit Test A low-level technical test focusing on small parts of a software system that can be executed quickly and in isolation. The definition and boundaries of a "unit" generally depends on the context and is to be agreed upon by the Development Team.

V

Velocity An optional, but often used, indication of the average amount of Product Backlog turned into an Increment of Product during a Sprint by a Scrum Team. Tracked by the Development Team for use within the Scrum Team.

INDEX

U
Ulwick, Tony, 27
unavailable Product Owners, 91–92
updating Product Backlog, 83–85

V
validating Product Backlog, 14,
    35–37
Value Areas, 26–27
value delivery, connecting PBIs
    (Product Backlog Items) to,
    51–52
values (Scrum), 28, 131–132

VCF (Virtual Case File) project, 113
velocity, visualizing, 63–64
versioned API management, 26
Virtual Case File (VCF) project, 113
visibility, planning, 65

W-X-Y-Z
Waterfall approach, mixing with
    Scrum, 107–108
What Customers Want (Ulwick), 27
work versus progress, 90–91
World Café method, 103
Zuill, Woody, 49

Credits

Page 4, Figure 1-1: The Scrum Framework. The Scrum framework is documented in the Scrum Guide, which is available, free of charge, at http://www.scrumguides.org/.

Page 8, Figure 2-1: The Nexus Framework for scaling Scrum. Nexus™ Framework © Scrum.org.

Page 9, Figure 2-1: Nexus Roles, Events, and Artifacts. Scrum.org.

Page 11, Figure 2-2: The NIT is accountable for maximizing the value of the Integrated Product. Scrum.org.

Page 11, Figure 2-3: Members of the NIT are usually drawn from Scrum Teams. Scrum.org.

Page 14, Figure 2-4: Nexus Sprint Planning. Scrum.org

Page 33, Figure 3-3: The NIT is composed of members of the Scrum Teams plus the Product Owner. Scrum.org.

Page 45, Figure 4-5: Visualizing dependencies using a cross-team refinement board. Scrum.org.

Page 48, Figure 4-6: "Sprint Planning in a Nexus at a Glance." Scrum.org.

Page 53, Figure 4-9: The Nexus uses the Nexus Sprint Backlog to manage the flow of work. Scrum.org.

Page 69, Figure 5-5: The Nexus Sprint Retrospective process. Scrum.org.

Page 131, Figure 8-1: Scrum values. Scrum.org.

Page 114, Figure 7-5: Emoji icons, emoticons for rate of satisfaction level. Five grade smileys for using in surveys. Colored and outline icons. Isolated illustration on white background. Sparkus Design/Shutterstock.

Register Your Product at informit.com/register

Access additional benefits and **save 35%** on your next purchase

- Automatically receive a coupon for 35% off your next purchase, valid for 30 days. Look for your code in your InformIT cart or the Manage Codes section of your account page.

- Download available product updates.

- Access bonus material if available.*

- Check the box to hear from us and receive exclusive offers on new editions and related products.

Registration benefits vary by product. Benefits will be listed on your account page under Registered Products.

InformIT.com—The Trusted Technology Learning Source

InformIT is the online home of information technology brands at Pearson, the world's foremost education company. At InformIT.com, you can:

- Shop our books, eBooks, software, and video training
- Take advantage of our special offers and promotions (informit.com/promotions)
- Sign up for special offers and content newsletter (informit.com/newsletters)
- Access thousands of free chapters and video lessons

Connect with InformIT—Visit informit.com/community

the trusted technology learning source

Addison-Wesley · Adobe Press · Cisco Press · Microsoft Press · Pearson IT Certification · Prentice Hall · Que · Sams · Peachpit Press

 Pearson